A Gift is for Giving

A Gifted Teacher's Lessons

MARILYN WICKSTROM

ISBN: 979-8-88640-630-6 (sc)
ISBN: 979-8-88640-631-3 (hc)
ISBN: 979-8-88640-632-0 (e)

THE EWINGS PUBLISHING

One Galleria Blvd., Suite 1900, Metairie, LA 70001
1-888-421-2397

CONTENTS

Section 2
Intruduction to Curriculum

INTRODUCTION

Our lives lead us into unforeseen pathways that build new horizons and fulfill dreams that were never part of our conscious reality. The mountains that are laid before us move and victories are gifts to lives we never knew or expected to know. As years evaporate into memories and we look over the challenges that have been blessings in disguise, we see a purpose beyond what we could have ever imagined.

Being a teacher for gifted students for over 27 years was an unexpected journey that could never have been planned, yet it was meant to be, and it was a gift that enlarged my capacity to grow and comprehend life from many new and enlightening perspectives.

I loved every day, every student, and every opportunity. As you travel through the pages that follow you will learn more about me and the circumstances that helped shape my values as an educator, and how they enhanced my abilities to embody the qualities that were so necessary to impart to my students.

When a child qualifies for the gifted program his or her life changes. While it is a wonderful validation of their learning capacity it is not a key to a perfect future. For those who are evaluated and do not meet the criteria that would welcome them into the Gifted arena there can be deep disappointment which can lead to life altering feelings of inadequacy and failure.

The whole scenario can be an incredibly complex and complicated world that elevates some and humbles others. When writing this book, I discovered I was able to verbalize feelings, emotions and convictions that streamed out from an inner fountain just waiting to be unleashed. I hope you find useful ideas that will help you unearth and interpret your own life.

In the scramble of parental egos and children who react to the expectations set before them, there is an incredible amount of good. Despite all the pressure, wonderful things are happening. May we be less apt to judge and more able to give and enjoy the exceptional qualities of each child. We need to help each child discover their unique profoundly important talents, whether they fall into the gifted category or not. We need to teach ourselves as well as our children to appreciate who they are and what they have to offer. And we must support them with the knowledge that they have gifts worth contributing to a world that needs them.

Part of this book is a group of activities that helped create the backbone of the class I taught. This information could be useful to homeschooled parents, any general education teacher who has the freedom to intermingle their own ideas with those required in the classroom, and of course to gifted teachers as well. The information is from years of experience and learning. I hope this book proves to be useful to everyone who reads it. It has been a revelation and joy to write.

ACKNOWLEDGEMENTS

The 27 years I taught the gifted program at Safety Harbor Elementary was a gift. My life has been blessed by the outstanding students and their families who filled my heart with love and joy. This book is a way for me to gratefully give back some of the good I have been given.

I want to thank Bobbi and my sister Barbara St. John for helping with the typing. I would also like to thank Karen Lieberman, PhD, for editing the manuscript and my wonderful husband for his patience, dedication, support and tireless hours of work in helping to put this book together. Most of the names have been changed.

CHAPTER 1

MY SON AND THE GIFTED PROGRAM

The straight back wooden chair made the wait even more uncomfortable. Nervous, I tried to read a magazine about educating children in inner-city schools. My eyes sped across the page, blurring the words. Finally, the door in front of me opened. The school psychologist, Mr. Snodgrass, said in a deep clinical voice, "Well, we completed the testing. Come in. Let's discuss the results."

My third-grade son, Daniel, stepped out from behind Mr. Snodgrass. He looked timid and insecure. I connected with his big brown eyes and gave him a reassuring smile. The room was small with grimy beige walls. A soft spray of sunshine from a window was the only redeeming light.

"Please, sit down Mrs. Wickstrom." He pointed to a chair next to the desk. "Daniel, why don't you wait outside for a few minutes?"

"It's okay, honey. We'll be done soon. There're some *Highlight* magazines out there for you to read." I attempted to hug him. He shrank in embarrassment and pulled away from my arms. He left the room and closed the door behind him.

"Well now, let's look at Daniel's test," Mr. Snodgrass said with a cordial professional air. He sat down and peered over his dark-rimmed glasses at the papers neatly arranged in a pile.

"Daniel did fairly well today. As you probably know he needs a score of 130 or higher to qualify for the gifted program."

"What was his score?" I asked confidently, expecting that my son had easily qualified.

"He got 128."

My heart sank with disappointment. I knew Dan was gifted. He had to be!

"However, Mrs. Wickstrom," he continued. "Dan's results are very unusual. The intelligence test evaluates verbal and non-verbal ability. To get the overall score we combine the two. In most cases these numbers are comparatively close. This was not the case with Daniel." He showed me a graph of the verbal portion of the test placing Dan in the average range. He then pointed to the non-verbal area indicating a number comfortably above 130.

"It's extremely unusual to see such a lopsided score." His tone was steeped with amazement.

"I am recommending we place your son into the gifted program for two reasons. First, because of his high non-verbal ability, and second, we can also consider him for placement if he is within two percentage points of the mean, which is, as you know 130. Dan's score of 128 places him within that range. He will need three letters of recommendation. Do you think you can get three letters?" he asked. His eyebrows rose, and his forehead wrinkled into ripples and then softened with an accepting smile.

"Of course, we can get the letters," I said, melting with relief. I felt a sense of victory and assured him that we would get anything that was needed as soon as possible.

A month later, after the letters were written and turned in, the gifted teacher sent us the meeting notice that would place Dan into the gifted program. After we signed the necessary paperwork, Dan was officially a gifted student. I was thrilled. My intuition was right. Our son's intellectual superiority was vindicated. We celebrated that night with ice cream sundaes from Hagen Daz.

I was proud to join the elite group of parents whose children were "gifted."

A year later his fourth-grade teacher wrote on his report card, "Dan should be an all A student. The grades are not as important as the fact that, by not being serious, he is wasting a good mind. I hope he matures."

The following year his fifth-grade teacher wrote, "Dan is putting forth minimum effort just to get by. I would like to see his capabilities applied more to academics than entertainment." Another teacher wrote, "Many papers are getting lost and assignments forgotten." The worst report came from his gifted teacher who gave him an "N" in conduct, which stood for "needs improvement." He also received "Ns" in listening skills, following directions, using time wisely, working independently, and being responsible.

I longed to see a report card like the one he received from his kindergarten teacher who gave him almost all "Es" (Excellent) with the comment, "Dan is a joy to have in class."

Being a member of the gifted program aligned Dan with the automatic expectation of excellence. He was not willing to be pushed into that role. The students who were recognized as outstanding leaders were on the principal's list or honor roll. They did more than what was expected and followed the rules, which brought them into harmony with their teacher's expectations. Dan sizzled inside at the thought of being a "goody-goody." That scene alienated him to the core. The gifted class was not responsible for his uncooperative attitude, but neither did it offer him an alternative for success. It only added to his problems by putting additional pressure on him to conform. Goofing around enabled him to defend his internal dignity and freed him from having to struggle with standards he didn't respect or accept. It also set him on a path that put him at odds with everyone in authority including his parents.

A heavy sense of failure began to invade my thoughts. It came with a sickening fear of defeat. I began to realize that Dan would never shine as a gifted student. He did, however, enjoy the creative activities in the class and loved the unstructured environment, so we kept him in the program. He continued to find his outlet by fooling around and letting everyone know that he didn't care.

Dan never yelled or argued with anyone. He silently and stubbornly ignored the things we expected him to do. When he completed his homework, we placed it in his backpack. He never turned it in to his teacher. He purposely lost notes that were sent home, making us unaware of his assignments or impending field trips. He loved the Nintendo, and spent countless hours playing Space Invaders with a neighbor instead of doing his homework. In desperation, we disconnected the game. We subscribed to the cable network, which included many adult channels— all of which we blocked using "Parental Controls." He would sneak out of his bedroom at night after we were asleep to play Nintendo and found a way to twist the television dial so he could see the adult programs. We had no choice but to cancel our cable subscription.

My sister saw how frustrated and upset I was over the situation and felt the growing tension between us. She was single without any financial obligations and offered to help with his schoolwork by paying $20 for each A, $15 for each B, and $10 for each C. Although it motivated him to bring up his grades, he remained distant and stubbornly rejected anything we cared about or valued.

His attitude in school separated him from the students who were motivated to get good grades and grouped him with those classmates that encouraged his disdainful disregard for authority.

School was an unhappy place for Dan. He found no success or support from anyone. He had only himself to blame, yet I desperately hoped for a miracle person to come, one who would care enough about him to recognize the goodness inside of him. It never happened.

When he turned fifteen, he got a job at a fast food restaurant. I was happy and relieved to see him doing something constructive. His boss praised him for his excellent work ethic. His dedication and responsible attitude amazed me. When he turned sixteen, he purchased a car. He had not consulted us or asked for money or advice.

As the years went by, the boys who Dan hung out with got into drugs and alcohol. Dan went along with them. More than once I emptied a whiskey bottle down the toilet. He was eventually caught with marijuana in high school and was expelled. The following year he took the initiative to reenroll so that he could graduate. It wasn't easy for him to return to school and face the students and teachers who knew his troubled background with drugs.

My husband and I took parenting classes to improve our communication and discipline skills. As hard as we tried, nothing seemed to work.

We literally forced Dan to go to church with us every Sunday and Wednesday evening. He enjoyed the activities of a two-week religious camp each summer.

We got him involved with other activities outside of school, which introduced him to children who were positive role models. He was not interested. We hired a counselor who worked with troubled teenagers. In the end, he learned by experiencing the consequences of his choices. He saw that drugs only got him into trouble. His friends were without high school diplomas. They couldn't hold a job and only focused on getting and using drugs. Dan was dominated by a driving desire for money. He saved every dollar he earned, waiting for his wallet to bulge with bills. Once that was accomplished, he would go out and splurge on brand name clothes like Polo shirts and New Balance shoes. We tried to encourage him to go to college, never dreaming that he would enroll in a trucking school without our knowledge. He worked out the financial details on his own. We were never asked to pay a penny.

The chemical truck he ended up driving turned over on the freeway. It was a miracle he didn't get hurt. He was taken to a nearby hospital to make sure there were no broken bones. We only found out about the incident when a friend showed us the picture of his truck along with his name in the *Tampa Tribune*. After the accident, he lost his job. He eventually moved to Chicago with his girlfriend, Sue. By that time, he was completely on his own, and we had learned to accept his choices. We let him know we loved him unconditionally. One night as he was sitting in a bar with Sue, she mockingly took his lighter and set his hair on fire. Horrified, a girl sitting near them took a napkin and pressed it against Dan's head, putting out the fire. She immediately caught Dan's attention. Her name was Meg. She was a musical theater major in college and came from a family and lifestyle that was like our own.

Something inside Dan came alive. He was looking at the girl who saved his hair from burning and who would, after three years of dating, become his wife. We were thrilled. Dan got a job in the information technology department at an international bank. He later became a vice president and is probably the only employee at his level without a college degree. The stubborn, independent qualities that got him into so much trouble when he was younger helped him overcome many obstacles. He is living the life he wanted.

I can humbly admit that despite all our efforts he is a self-made man. We got through some difficult years, but it ended up with each of us having a deep love and respect for the other. We have asked him if he regrets not going to college, and his answer is emphatically "No." School did not interest him. Dan sets his own goals. They are free from the pressures and expectations of others. It is the way he has always lived his life, and I doubt he will ever change. Our younger son fit naturally into the social structure of his gifted class. He had many friends and positive experiences in the gifted program. It has been a privilege to see him develop into a dedicated teacher who expresses his unique talents for understanding and patience in the classroom. He is also a wonderful, loving husband and father. His gifted I.Q. has contributed very little to his ability to find and give happiness in his life.

All this taught me that getting into a gifted program is not for everyone and not half as important as I thought it was. I asked myself if my own ego had forced me to push our son.

During the years I taught the gifted class, I saw many children who, like our son, did not fit into the norm. As parents we want the best for our children. We see them as perfect and wonderful. We sometimes set unrealistic expectations that challenge them beyond their working capacity. They feel our disappointment in them. The consequences of this can be devastating. My overbearing willfulness created a huge wall that stood between our son and our ideals. We should have encouraged Dan to be who he was, not who we wanted him to be. Speaking from experience, the label of "gifted" is not necessarily an open door to success.

The experiences I had with our son and the gifted program transformed my ideals as a mother. My aspirations for a perfect child were shattered as crushing waves of humility washed away mountains of pride. When I became a teacher in the gifted program, the lessons from the past came with me.

When most teachers teach, they have little awareness of what kind of environment they are creating in the classroom. Their focus is on the subject they are teaching. It is normal to appreciate those students who do well, say please and thank you, turn in their homework, and study for tests. They should get positive feedback because they deserve it. The students who do little to earn approval and are sloppy and disruptive also need positive encouragement. We are destroying the spirit of many of our promising students, and even if they don't seem to be doing well, their potential should be considered. After all, one could end up a vice president of a bank or teaching gifted students. Beneath every facade there is hope. We need to be sure that we are not taking away that hope or dimming someone's potential. Each student deserves an open door, even if it looks as if they will never walk through it. We need to make sure we are not closing doors in any faces.

Every good teacher yearns to satisfy the needs of all their children. I encouraged mine to believe in themselves. I tried to give my students freedom for self-discovery by offering them choices and opportunities to pursue their interests. More than anything, I wanted each one to know I cared. When I had a student that required more help than I was able to give, I struggled with a feeling of failure and discouragement. As the years went by, it was an astounding revelation to me that the very students I had been the most concerned with were the very ones that came back for a visit and to thank me for making a difference in their lives. They taught me never to judge who I was reaching. I had to keep doing my best and trying my hardest.

CHAPTER **2**

GETTING THE JOB

The position didn't float effortlessly into my life. I had interviewed for the job in August, but the principal, Mr. Hall, hired someone else with more experience. It was now September and school had been in session for almost three weeks.

Teaching at a Montessori school as an assistant was not giving me the chance to activate the gifted certification I had recently earned at USF. I felt misplaced and longed for the opportunity to use all the creative ideas caged inside my thwarted spirit.

Haunted by a constant inner prodding, I called the gifted supervisor on my lunch break.

"I hate to bother you, but I thought I would ask one more time if there is some opening to teach a gifted class in Pinellas County?"

"You know that position at Safety Harbor Elementary is open." My heart leaped in amazed anticipation.

"The woman Mr. Hall hired took another job. He needs someone to fill that vacancy. Why don't you call him?"

In less than five minutes, I was talking with Mr. Hall explaining that I had a job working at a Montessori school, but really wanted to teach gifted.

"Come over after school today at five and we can talk." His voice was polite but not encouraging.

Hours couldn't move fast enough that afternoon. At long last the children were dismissed, and I was free to leave. I couldn't be late. I wove my car from one lane to another, looking for a break in the heavy stream of traffic moving down U.S. 19. I arrived five minutes before five. As I turned into the school parking lot a foreboding insecurity and fear knotted my stomach. One-third of me wanted to turn around and go home, but the other two-thirds was never going to let that happen. I knew I belonged here, but I didn't know why.

The lot was completely empty except for one Jeep Cherokee parked in the space marked "Principal." I pulled up beside it, got out of the car and proceeded to the side door, which was still open. I walked up the cement stairs into the silent hallway. Mr. Hall's light was the only sign of life. He was sitting in his office with piles of papers strewn across his desk. A two-liter bottle of Coke sat in the middle of the mess. He looked up and gave me a tired smile. Prepared to be riddled with questions, I was surprised when he stood up, grabbed his keys, and motioned for me to follow him up the stairs. He unlocked a dark wooden door that had been given many coats of glossy shellac through the years. It opened to a vacant classroom. Mr. Hall's words bounced off the walls and smooth oak tables like a voice echoing in a cave that hadn't seen life in a thousand years.

"This will be your room. You'll need some supplies, obviously. It's empty in here. We have a warehouse supply catalog in the office that you can get from our secretary, Marge. Get to know her. She will help with what you need."

He pointed to two soft covered books on the desk. "Mrs. Procter left these for her replacement. She told me that it would be enough to get you started."

Mr. Hall looked away from me and stared at the floor. The books were thin. One was about dinosaurs; the other about future cities. There was nothing else. Mr. Hall's soft brown eyes looked directly into mine, "There is a lot to learn, Marilyn, and you may find this whole thing more difficult that you anticipated. Be patient with yourself." The compassion in his voice let me feel like I had his support and understanding. I didn't have the slightest clue as to what this job entailed or what he was referring to as "difficult." Whatever it was, I was ready to give it all that I had, and I couldn't wait to get started.

"Here are the keys to your room. Take the rest of the week to let the Montessori school know you're leaving. Monday will be your first day. You're new to the county. You will need to fill out extra paperwork. We want to get you started as soon as possible."

I wanted to hug him and jump through the ceiling with joy. Heaven was real and at that moment it had found me. I thanked him, trying to hold back my excitement with dignified restraint. I drove home on a cloud of jubilation. I couldn't wait to tell my family. Over the next two days, I wrapped up my responsibilities at the Montessori school. I told them I was sorry, and they said they would miss me. The door was open to come back and teach an after-school enrichment class. I thanked them for the opportunity but knew I would be too focused on my new job to make that happen.

Monday morning finally came. I was anxious to meet my students and to be a contributing addition to my new school.

After I signed the attendance roster, I headed up the stairs to my room. I saw my first student. She was standing with her mother at the drinking fountain across from the gifted classroom. "Hello," came a low voice that was steeped with the smoothness of chamomile tea in desperate need of a minimum of three heaping tablespoons of sugar.

"My name is Joyce Wiggins." Dressed like the office manager that she was, her tightly fitting grey suit stretched over her short, round figure. Her black hair was trimmed neatly and lay flatly against her head. Her dark probing brown eyes were anything but warm or accepting in nature.

"I want you to meet my daughter, Joy. She will be in your third-grade class this year. Joy looked like her mother's twin with twenty years of growth separating their identical features. Her expression had a coy cockiness that was void of friendliness or warmth.

"Hi," I said expecting a response, but there was none. How, I wondered, could an eight-year-old child look so amazingly intelligent and act so rude at the same time?

"We all loved Mrs. Procter. You know of course that she was an excellent gifted teacher," Mrs. Wiggins continued. "She's the best!" Her words were not half as cutting as the bitterness in which they were spoken.

"I've heard that she was very well liked," I replied, attempting to maintain an attitude of conciliation. It was obvious that this woman was experiencing a great sense of loss with Mrs. Procter's exit. I tried to be understanding and to identify with her feeling of regret while communicating an encouraging tone of my own.

Joy went to the water fountain and turned on the water. It rose up in a bubbling, streaming arch that rolled down the drain making the sound of an empty stomach growling during a Sunday morning church service. Mrs. Wiggins ignored her daughter's deliberate attempt to get attention and said, "Mrs. Procter will be teaching at Purdue University this fall. We thought we would like to take a trip up there to see her. We all hated to see her go. Seven years—that's how long she was here at Safety Harbor. We were so lucky to have her teach our Joy." She paused and then looked directly into my eyes. "What experience do you have teaching gifted children, Mrs. Wickstrom?" The accusing sound of her voice drilled away my confidence with supreme accuracy. This was not the way I had envisioned my first moments of my first day. I hadn't even had a chance to unlock the door of my classroom. Undoubtedly, she would view my credentials as disappointing.

"I'm new at teaching gifted students. I just received my certification this past summer. I'm looking forward to getting to know everyone. I've been out of the classroom for fifteen years." I wondered why I had offered that last unnecessary detail. My chest ached for someplace to breathe and my stomach felt like a balloon ready to explode. How was I ever going to live up to Mrs. Procter's reputation? I looked at Mrs. Wiggins; she was staring at me and not saying a word. I was judged before I even got started.

"I'm so glad you came up to meet me, Mrs. Wiggins. I'm looking forward to having you in class, Joy." After shaking both their hands firmly, I unlocked the door to my room and closed it behind me. I fell into the nearest chair like a loosely stuffed scarecrow. The sun was just rising over the row of houses across the street from the school. The room's emptiness was filled with new light and hope for better moments to come. My future with the Wiggins' would have a happy ending. It took a while, however, to overcome the battlefield of first impressions that ignited itself with insecurity in that hallway. Teaching would not only be a chance to inspire and enrich the lives of my students, it would become a victory lap for driving over my fears and crushing the negative remnants of my past.

To get to know my students, I interviewed each of them individually. I wanted to know what they liked about the gifted class, and what their interests were.

I took the first group of students from Mrs. Stricture's fifth grade. Walking into her class felt like being in a courtroom governed by a high executioner. She was a tough disciplinarian whose shrill voice cut through any opposition like a hot knife in butter. It didn't matter what time of the day you entered her room—morning, mid-morning, afternoon, or just before dismissal. Her students were silent and sitting upright at their desks. I was just as afraid of her as they were. I asked to speak to Allison Miller. The two of us walked quietly down the hall to my classroom and sat at a long table where I began to write notes. "What things did you like about being in gifted?" I asked, trying to act casual and informal enough to make her feel at ease. Without hesitation she responded, "Field trips." This answer was repeated many times as I talked with other students. I learned that they had visited the Thomas Edison Museum in Ft. Meyers, The Museum of Science and Industry in Tampa, and the Kennedy Space Center on the east coast. I asked about the subjects they had studied. They had mapped out the trip of Lewis and Clark and had learned about the Inca and Aztec Indians. Mark loved the math. Willie couldn't get enough of the puzzles and mazes. Rebecca was non-comital and seemed willing to follow any idea or subject. Christina was a perfectionist and loved art, all of which served her well as an architect. Joshua's father was a minister. Dave wanted to be a lawyer like his father. Julie's father was an engineer and worked at a nearby flight simulation center, where she said we could go on a field trip.

One of the more open students was Morgen. He was new to Safety Harbor and never had Mrs. Procter. This made it much easier to connect with him. He was an excellent public speaker, and later set up his own law office. It was difficult getting the students to open up. They sat waiting for me to ask the questions, which they would answer with a few words. They were hesitant to talk about themselves or the things they did after school. It was obvious by their distant attitudes that they were not at all happy to get familiar with someone new. They felt abandoned. I could feel their disappointment. I soon saw that these children were as diverse as any group of children anywhere. Getting to know them as individuals was something I longed for. These interviews put me on the first step toward this goal. I also wanted to know their parents, realizing I was going to be an influence in their home life by the assignments they would bring home each week. I needed to know as much about their families as possible. I saw my job as more than a six-hour-a-day commitment. It was to support and help form the development of each student into a contributing member of our society and world. Their lives would soon be part of mine. Through the years I had brothers, sisters, and cousins. There were two students whose grandmother had been a close high school friend of mine. As the years went by, I taught children of my former students, as well. It was a world I would cherish and honor.

After I finished talking to the students, I looked around the empty room. I had no idea about the wonderful experiences that were to come or of the challenges that lay ahead.

How was I ever going to fill the vacancy of this excellent teacher? Mr. Hall told me, "You will never have the fifth graders. You have a chance with the fourth grade. Your first, second, and third grade students will be yours. Just give them time."

The classroom was stripped from top to bottom. Mrs. Procter had taken every book, paper, and teaching tool with her. The two paper book manuals that sat on the teacher's desk were all that I had. I couldn't help but wonder how such a beloved teacher could leave so little for the students she left behind.

On the south side of my room was a connecting door to the music class. Barb Nichols was the teacher. Barb was a single woman about my age. She had short light brown hair and a big smile. Music was her passion, but standing in front of an audience directing her students threw her off emotionally. Fearing something would go wrong or the performance would not live up to her standards, she was in a constant state of nervous frustration before every concert. Barb was very popular with the staff and had a close-knit group of friends at school. One day she shared with me her thoughts about the gifted program. "It's an exclusive group of stuck-up kids and their pushy parents," she said resentfully. "They act like they are better than everybody else. They walk around school in their own world. They don't respect teachers or try to support anything outside their own precious gifted clique. Mrs. Procter was responsible for it all. She just cared about her own smart little angels. We were all glad to see her go." She looked at me with a questioning gaze trying to determine my reaction to the words that were spilling out of her mouth.

"Things are going to change, Barb," I told her. I was determined to prove that she would be pleasantly surprised by the attitudes coming from the students in my class. She gave me a smile that told me she was waiting to see it happen. It didn't take long for me to experience the same concerns from the rest of the staff. To get to know the other teachers in the school, I made it a point to eat lunch in the lounge. My presence was met by unfriendly coolness. Stares and critical glances greeted me as I sat down at the table filled with teachers. "So, you have those smart alecks—good luck!"

"Why would anyone want to teach those brats?"

"Better be ready for those parents. They will be on your case all year long."

"I suppose you will take them on trips the rest of the school can't go on." I didn't have the answers for all the complaints. The only thing I could do was change the attitude of my classes. I would show everyone in school that the gifted kids were great kids, and their parents were helpful and indispensable to our progress as a forward-moving school.

Everyone was busy with their own responsibilities. I was isolated at the far end of the school. There was no reason for anyone to include me in any activities. Barb was the only teacher I talked to. Due to some conflicts with a new principal, she and three of her close friends transferred to another school. Safety Harbor missed her excellent performances and professionalism. I lost a good friend.

During the year we were both at Safety Harbor, she never complained about the gifted class again.

I was on a mission. How could the gifted students become ambassadors for good in their school? This superior attitude was not going to continue on my watch. I could understand why Mr. Hall had not been eager to fill my position. He wanted to avoid the antagonism and criticism that was now mine to handle. I felt like a sparrow in an army of blue jays. Somehow, we would find a way to fly together harmoniously.

I became dedicated to teaching my students that everyone was gifted, but in different ways. No one was better than anyone else. I encouraged my classes to appreciate the special gifts in everyone. Some people were experts in math; some shone in reading, science, or sports. I also wanted the children to recognize the special gifts of kindness and philanthropy. Their successes in life did not rely on IQ scores. They came from the willingness to share the gifts they were given. I constantly tried to instill a desire in them to care for their world and all the people in it. We had a class motto: A gift is for giving.

CHAPTER 3

THE TEACHER I BECAME

You know something is right, but you don't know why. You feel yourself being directed to a path that defies all logic. Yet you allow yourself to be carried beyond horizons that your imagination could never have believed possible. The world that was now mine to embrace placed me on an unknown and uncharted territory. Who would have guessed?

Standing in my new classroom at Safety Harbor Elementary I had the title "Teacher of the Gifted." I thought back to when I was five years old. My kindergarten teacher had given my class the assignment to memorize and recite a rhyme. I was ready with one I had made up myself. Proudly I presented the words, "I bit my tongue chewing my gum." Everyone laughed. The poem impressed my teacher enough to place me in the first-grade class of quick learners. I wouldn't have known I had been elevated to such a distinctive level had it not been for one ego shattering experience. My new teacher asked me a question I didn't understand. It all happened over sixty-five years ago, but I can still remember the sharp impatient tone of her voice as her words shot over the entire classroom.

"How did you ever get into this class?" Her words sent shock waves of embarrassment and shame into every inch of my body. I wanted to cry, but fear overtook my shattered emotions. The next day she told me I had been placed in a new class. I knew why. I wasn't smart like everyone in my old class.

As the years went by, I became aware that the high achieving students were in a group in which I didn't belong. They were the teachers' helpers. They were the kids whose mothers drove on field trips, brought gifts for the teachers, and got to wear pretty clothes. They were the ones who raised their hands with all the right answers.

By the time I got into high school, I had adjusted to feeling inferior, but I kept trying to improve. I joined a lot of clubs including the yearbook staff. One day my counselor called me into his office. He was a gentle soft-spoken man, popular and well respected by everyone. His opinion was important. I believed him wise and kind. I came into his office and sat down in a chair next to his desk as he opened a file sporting my name on the outside.

"Marilyn," he said in a deep, sincere voice. "You are getting close to graduating. I would recommend that you don't waste your time going to college. Your test scores indicate that you would be much happier as a shop clerk. College would be much too difficult for you. You'd have to work twice as hard just to get by." I stared at him but couldn't speak. Stepping out of his office with my books clenched to my chest, rebellion raged inside me. I would go to college no matter what this well-intentioned man or anyone else said. I didn't care what he thought. I knew he was wrong, and I was going to prove it.

It might have helped that my parents were alumni of the small liberal arts college, Olivet. Whatever the reason, I was accepted with a C+ high school average.

The campus was situated among rolling grass lined hills and sprawling oak trees that had seen more history than the small college town itself.

The girl's dormitory had a wide-open staircase leading up to the rooms on the second and third floors. My mother helped carry my suitcases from the car. When we got to the room, she sat me down and looked into my eyes. "These will be the best years of your life." Love and emotion streamed from her voice as memories surged in the forefront of her mind. Leaning over me she held my head in her hands and kissed me goodbye.

Alone to demonstrate the dreams I was determined to fulfill, I was on my way to independence and success. The fear of failure helped steer me away from the social life I had prioritized in high school.

It didn't take long to realize that the dormitory was no place to do class assignments. Music blared from rooms and hovered through the halls like a scan button on the radio. Girls roamed through the halls looking for random conversations. The library had a quiet room that turned into my sanctuary before and after dinner. It gave me refuge for self-discipline and my development as a serious student. My first challenge was a world history class taught by a young idealistic professor that lectured exclusively from his own personal notes. Half the class was failing. The remaining half complained about the difficult demands he made on them. Mr. Hubbard wove historical figures and events into a tapestry of evolving philosophies. I was used to reading books and answering questions at the end of each chapter. I routinely memorized places and dates for tests each week. Nothing prepared me for the expectations of this class.

Gratefully, I discovered a friend who had taken a similar course in a junior college the year before. The credits had not transferred, and she was required to repeat the class. The two of us found an empty room where we could study without being distracted. We went through our notes together, discussing each factor that helped create change. Kathy and I became immersed on our journey through time. We talked all night and well into the next morning without a break. Learning to analyze, think, and understand the flow of change put learning on a whole different level.

Art classes also contributed to my intellectual development. The minute my brush connected with the canvas I knew I was home and captured by an inner expression of creative inspiration.

My instructor took a very low-key approach to teaching. He rarely gave a group lesson on how to paint. Mr. Balner sat at his desk in a corner of the room and let us explore our individual approach to painting. Occasionally he made suggestions or told us to look up a specific artist if he thought we could learn from their particular style. The class met twice a week on Tuesday and Thursday from 2:00 to 4:00 P.M. The time evaporated. I could often be found leaving the art studio at 7:00 P.M., treating myself to an ice cream cone dinner as I walked back to the dorm in the dark.

Our field trip to the Toledo Museum of Fine Arts amazed me. Impressionism was my heart's desire. I didn't want to leave the paintings. I wanted to analyze the way the paint was applied and to understand the magical way that life danced in subtle rainbows of color capturing the soft mist of a sunlit day. It was love at first sight.

With worlds of knowledge opening to me, I was discovering who I was and what was important. I loved taking walks to the post office on a small out of the way path behind the girls' dormitory. It wound around an open meadow. Wild flowers sprinkled above high waving grass. Tall white flakes of Queen Anne's lace brought golden butterflies fluttering in the sunshine while field birds chattered their sweet songs. I began to appreciate the perfectly balanced canvas of nature. The landscape was glorified with varying colors, textures, and priceless beauty. It was like a prayer to my soul, and I cherished the peace and solitude.

I had been like a pond, empty and parched dry, bursting to be filled without knowing it. Waterfalls of ideas came plunging into my mind enriching and awakening my thought into whirlpools of profound exultation. I embraced each learning experience with joy.

At the end of my sophomore year I felt alive and free. Never, I thought, did I ever want to lose the knowledge I held inside. Learning was an incredible gift, and I never wanted to let it go. Nothing would be more important to me than to share this enthusiasm with my future students. It wasn't the accumulation of facts. It was the process of discovery—the inspiration and desire to know more and to enjoy the journey.

I transferred to a larger college in my junior year. The curriculum was more focused on practical applications of knowledge. The opportunities and excitement I enjoyed at Olivet faded in the background.

It took fifteen years. I was married and the mother of two boys. The world I never dreamed would be mine was becoming a reality as

I prepared to teach gifted children. Who would have guessed? Like so much of my life, success didn't come easily. I looked at the room stripped of paper, books, and pencils. Being the only teacher of gifted in the school gave me complete freedom, but it also deprived me of any guidance or assistance. I was on my own with no idea of what to do or how to do it. I accepted this opportunity because I felt an unquestionable pull to do so. I was an art education major, but I didn't want to just teach art. The world was too full of interesting subjects to learn and share with my students. I wanted to explore so much more than art. I longed to know my students, so I could help and encourage them in their learning experiences. Having them for one full day each week offered me a much greater opportunity to make a meaningful impact on their lives. I wasn't limited to a prescribed curriculum. I was free to teach anything in any way I thought appropriate. This unlimited scope was exciting. I couldn't wait to get started.

For all the years I spent growing up, feeling inferior to my classmates, I would now be a leader and an inspiration to gifted students. My background helped me to help them appreciate and see good in everyone. As the years went by, I shared a bond with my students and their families. Whenever someone complemented me as an exceptionally intelligent person, I smiled inside. Life teaches lessons. Our abilities come from our love of giving and in our ability to open hearts to leadership from others. Every storm feeds the hungry and plants gardens of unplanned beauty.

CHAPTER 4

QUESTIONABLE PLACEMENT

An intelligence test is not something that you pass or fail. It is a measurement of your cultural awareness, logical reasoning, and memory skills. It does not assess a student's desire to work hard and do their best.

Many parents who were devastated when their children did not qualify tried to overturn the results. They would call the gifted supervisor, for example, and complain that their child did not feel well on the day of the test. They claimed they were not told in advance of the testing and that their child did not get enough sleep the night before. They complained that the psychologist was mean and intimidating. Some wealthier parents paid hundreds of dollars to have their child retested by a private psychologist who helped the child qualify for the program. Some of the children who were retested became wonderful additions to the class. Unfortunately, others had difficulty keeping up. These children began to lose their self-confidence. Helping them achieve success without downgrading the instruction level of the class was a constant challenge.

One young boy who should never have been placed in the gifted program was Mark. He had short black hair that was immaculately trimmed to showcase his gentle brown eyes. Freckles splashed across his nose and healthy pink cheeks. A soft kindness embraced his presence, giving him an innocence that made me want to protect him from hurt or disappointment. He was like a sleeping sea turtle drifting in the middle of frolicking dolphins.

Mark was able to qualify for the gifted program after a private psychologist tested him. Mark may have had a learning disability, but he was never evaluated for that possibility. He was a deep thinker, but struggled with emotional insecurity. He interpreted his mistakes as inadequacy. If he had been more self-motivated and surer of himself to start with, he could have had a more positive experience in the gifted class and in everything he did. To see him struggle to maintain a positive status with his peers was agonizing. He longed for their acceptance yet feared he would look inferior if he spoke up and expressed an opinion.

He had come to Safety Harbor Elementary from Leila Davis Elementary because of a change in the school zoning—a convenient escape from his former gifted teacher, who I later discovered had been taking steps to remove him from the program. Mark had skillfully learned to become invisible in class. He never talked, raised his hand, or did anything to draw attention to himself in any way. This tactic deprived him of learning and asking crucial questions. Somehow, he had concluded that he could work up to the level of his gifted classmates.

To avoid embarrassing moments, he mentally withdrew from his class altogether. Several years of this behavior had saddled him with an introverted fear of failure.

The gravity of the situation hit me one day when, after collecting logic puzzles, I found a nameless paper that was totally illegible. Scribbled words streaked the paper like lightning across a night summer sky. I checked off the papers in my grade book and accounted for every student except Mark. The anonymous paper had to be his. To cover his inability to understand his work, he had thrashed lines all over his paper making it impossible to read. This was an old but familiar trick, one I tried once or twice in my grade school years. It never worked for me then, and it wasn't going to work for Mark now.

The following week, when his class came to gifted, I called him to my desk.

"Is this your paper, Mark?" I asked, keeping my voice low and confidential. His eyes quickly turned away from me and nervously searched the room to see if anyone was listening.

"No," he said emphatically clenching his fist and shuffling his feet nervously on the floor.

My purpose was not to embarrass him. I only wanted to give him the help he needed. I decided not to push the subject. Instead, I took the new puzzle and read it to him and explained how to work it out. He examined the ceiling, his body shaking. The situation had worked itself into a problem that couldn't be easily solved. His anxiety clearly showed that he didn't want to give the slightest hint that he needed help. That day when I collected papers from the class, he hid his and asked if he could take it home to complete. Earlier that day I had found him putting his name on someone else's paper.

After lunch each week our class congregated on the carpet in what was called "the gathering area." This time gave the students a chance to share with one another. Trips to Disney World, family events, and sporting events were popular topics. I especially enjoyed listening to students who had taken the time to research information about animals and places around the world. The students got to know and care about one another through this interaction. It also gave them a chance to practice their speaking and listening skills. I made a point to include everyone in these discussions.

Mark's class was large and full of active, verbal children who were more than willing to dominate the discussion. Because of this, I often chose certain students to speak even if they didn't raise their hands. Mark scrunched behind as many people as he could find to avoid taking part in this activity. I didn't want to make him feel uncomfortable, but this was a chance for him to share without being afraid of making a mistake. He needed to be encouraged, and he needed to feel success.

"Mark," I said. "We would like to hear from you. What would you like to share?" He froze. His eyes desperately searched for another student named Mark. He was out of luck.

"Do you play sports?" I asked in order to help him.

"Yes."

"What do you play?"

"Baseball."

"What position do you play?"

"I pitch." His voice wavered.

"How did your last game go?"

"Our team won." A smile spread over his face as he continued. "The score was five to four. Our team was ahead. It was the ninth inning, and my arm was aching like crazy. But I didn't care. We had to win this game. We just had to win. So we could be in the playoffs. My team was counting on me. I had to pitch the best I ever could. I couldn't let them down. I just couldn't. Everyone kept shouting 'Mark, Mark you can do it Mark.'" He took a deep breath. "I did it. It was the ninth inning, and I struck out all three batters. One, Two, Three batters—boom! We won the game. We won." Mark's face was radiant.

"I felt bad for the team that lost. I told them I was sorry, but we get to go to the playoffs, and I helped my team."

Chills spread all over my body. To see Mark so excited and animated was amazing. His victory was not just in helping his team win, it was in overcoming his fear of speaking up and taking an active part in his class.

"That is absolutely wonderful, Mark. Your team must be absolutely thrilled to have you as their pitcher," I said, hoping that he would feel my genuine support for his accomplishments. He gave me a self-conscious grin. Mark would have more moments like the one he had just experienced. I was determined to make that happen. He had risen a notch higher in everyone's eyes that day and he knew it. Glimpsing into this part of Mark was gratifying.

Deep inside his silence was a motivated, sensitive, selfless young man buried under the weight and pressure that deprived him of his freedom and joy.

His general education teacher complained that he needed to be in his regular class. He was two years below grade level in reading. She couldn't understand how Mark had qualified for gifted in the first place. Missing one full day of instruction to go to the gifted program created a real problem. She had placed him at a table near her desk, so she could monitor his progress.

Mark's family lived in an exclusive gated community. His mother was a tall slender well-dressed woman with long blond hair that hung loosely on her shoulders. Having to tell her my concerns about keeping Mark in the gifted class was painful. Despite the advances we were making socially, I still had grave concerns for his academic progress not only in gifted, but also in his regular class as well.

She pleaded with me. "Mark's whole self-image will be destroyed if he is not in the gifted program." She shook her head with tears in her eyes. "You just can't do that! Please understand how important this is to him."

"Mark is so scared and insecure that he stutters and trembles every time I try to include him in class discussions," I said. "He doesn't complete his classwork."

Her stubborn willfulness shut out my words. Mark's participation in gifted was a problem, but because of his mother's pressure taking him out of the program was also a problem. This kind of situation, although extreme, was not unusual.

Mark did not want to disappoint his mother, but in his effort to please her he felt like a failure. What he needed was to have his mother accept him for who he was not who she wanted him to be.

I found a high school student to help him after school, and I let him take his unfinished work home. This made a big difference, but it did not solve the problem.

Then there was Linda—a soft spoken, beautiful young lady with long golden curls and sparkling brown eyes. She fit the classical stereotype of the ideal gifted student. She had been on the honor roll all through school. She was well-mannered, poised, and self-assured. Only one obstacle stood in her way. She could not get a qualifying score on the I.Q. test. She had been referred for testing in the gifted program by her teachers in kindergarten and third grade with the same disappointing results. Then, her younger brother, Stephen, was accepted into the program. She had struggled with discouraging test results all through grade school. Many of her friends were in the gifted class, but now that her brother was coming home with projects and field trip permission slips, she really wanted to become part of the excitement and fun.

Linda was in the fifth grade and wanted to try one last time. I sympathized with her motives, but was not at all sure that the testing results would give her the positive outcome she wanted. We went through with the testing, and for the third time Linda did not qualify.

She had a passion for music and dance. The school talent show gave her the opportunity to amaze her classmates with her exceptional singing voice. Her mother invited my husband and me to a special holiday rendition of The Nutcracker Suite. Linda's performance in this program was extraordinary. She went on to take a leading role in some high school musicals and majored in musical theater in college.

Linda found her passion. She is a shining example of someone who discovered that she didn't need to be in the gifted program for recognition and success. Her parents let her know that she was wonderful just the way she was, and it didn't matter to them if she was or wasn't in the gifted program.

It is difficult for parents who have one child who qualifies while the other does not.

Bradford and William, twins, were another example. Bradford scored very well on the I.Q. test. William did not qualify. His mother and father considered keeping Bradford out of the class, so William would not feel left out. In the end, they decided to retest William privately. He squeaked through, with three letters of recommendation. They thought their problems were over. Little did anyone realize that this was only the beginning of a much larger challenge. First, William knew his twin brother had scored higher than he had. Bradford had a strong personality. He was a natural leader and did not feel any responsibility for William or his feelings. He went out of his way to distance himself from his brother when they came to class. Being ignored by Bradford was one thing, but William was shunned by all the boys his brother hung out with. Bradford was popular. William was shy and alone. I could see him withdrawing. I split up the group that Bradford was with, changing their seats. I also talked with Bradford, asking him to include his brother in his group activities. I tried to encourage William to mix with the class. He felt unwanted and could not assert himself enough to contribute in group activities. He felt inferior to his brother. I saw the strengths in William's repertoire of abilities. He was artistic and loved opportunities that allowed his creative ideas to surface. He enjoyed working independently, but desperately needed the assurance that he was likeable and desired as a friend. If I could redo this story, I would not have put William in the program. He could have taken art lessons, played a musical instrument, or found an activity that he excelled in apart from Bradford. Finding ways to develop his talents could have given him the ability to grow independently. He could have found friends that shared similar interests. He needed to be in a situation where he was not compared with Bradford. This would have helped build his self-confidence.

Every situation is different, but it is imperative to recognize the individuality of each student. Trying to force brothers and sisters into the same gifted class because you don't want to hurt their feelings is not a good idea. It can cause deeper problems, which will foster inner resentment and affect the child's self-confidence for years to come.

CHAPTER 5

ATTITUDES

WHO IS IN CHARGE?

It happens to parents who are proud and impressed with their child's intelligence. It shows in the admiration they have for the way their son or daughter responds to their surroundings by doing amazing things. Neighbors, family members, aunts, uncles, and even grandparents all remark on how smart their children are. Time only concludes that you have an exceptionally valuable young genius on your hands. Next comes the child sensing that people think they are special, which, in many cases, makes them feel empowered. It is logical to expect special treatment, and if they don't get what they want, many times it results in a good old temper tantrum. This tactic is an attempt to gain attention and control, and it often works.

If I were to give advice to a parent of a gifted child employing this tactic, I would suggest they reflect seriously on this attitude. Being gifted is an academic gift, it does not include the character traits that will determine their success and/or happiness. Many adults struggle with these conflicts.

One such example occurred at a home for the elderly. They had hired a new employee as a manager. He was obviously intelligent and capable, but only lasted about three weeks. The problem was not his ability to do the job, it was in his superior attitude and inability to listen to the needs and ideas of others. His unwillingness to listen and cooperate with his staff made it impossible for him to continue in the position.

Children that are gifted are still children. They need to learn to accept authority and obedience. They need to be responsible and to contribute to their family. While they need to realize they have abilities that exceed what others have, they are not better than anyone else. They have been given a gift. A gift is for giving, it is not to feel superior, dictatorial, or willful. If we allow these attitudes to prevail and grow, we are doing the gifted child a disservice and in many ways depriving them of developing their full potential; self-absorption creates stagnation. Be hard on yourself, but be kind to your gifted child and help them learn to obey and respect your authority. The world does not revolve around them.

IT'S BORING

I can't begin to count the times I heard the phrase "It's boring." It is an insult to the teacher and an unkind remark to her students who are working on a project. I came to understand that if someone was bored, they were boring. They did not put forth any effort to make life or learning more interesting.

I challenged my students to make a "boring" assignment fun; nothing is boring if you put a creative spin on it. I told the class that learning was an adventure and a wonderful opportunity. If they thought something was below their ability, it was up to them to challenge themselves. If they had a math assignment that seemed repetitious, do it but include story problems or make it more difficult.

If they had to do a report about something they thought was boring, make the report a story. For example: If the assignment was asking how a volcano is formed, write about a rabbit experiencing the development of a volcano. If it was a science project on magnets, make a diorama.

There was always a way to make boring things interesting and fun. It all depended on their willingness to open their minds and find ways to be creative.

THE COVER-UP

What about the students that are just plain lazy and depend upon their parents to get them out of things they don't like or want to do?

Sometimes teachers can win; sometimes they lose. It is a fact of life, and as much as I hate to admit it, I have failed some of my students, not because I didn't try, but because the battle was not just with the child but with n the parent, as well.

One example was with a young girl whose mother was an assistant principal. I knew her because we had been friends before she transferred and was elevated to her position. Her daughter was in my class and was not excited to be there. She had friends and considered her day in gifted as her day off from work. I was not satisfied with her work, which was minimal at best.

The real problem came when I passed out the instructions for the yearly research report. This paper came with detailed instructions on how to organize the work. We read the paper thoroughly together in class, and I assigned a date for when the outline was due. When the due date came, the young lady did not have her report, nor did she have it the following week or the week after that. I called the mother, who assured me the paper would be done. The next week, it was still not done. I told her that if the report was not finished by the next class, she would have to go to the library and would not be allowed in class until she completed the paper.

I gave her detailed instructions on what to do; she did not do anything. I called her mother and again, she assured me the paper would be handed in the following week. Again, she came to class without her paper. She was back in the library once again. The next week she stayed in her regular class and did not come to gifted at all. After talking to the mother, it was decided to take her daughter out of the class, but her mother wanted to have her daughter in the gifted class for middle school. We settled on a meeting date for the mother to come and sign the necessary paperwork. She never came, so I put the necessary work together and finalized the papers without the mother's attendance.

Her desire to keep her daughter in the program was clear, but she was unable to discipline her daughter, control the child's stubborn attitude, or to complete the paperwork, which would allow the child back into the program. She was not doing her daughter any favors. There was an obvious power struggle going on and the daughter had won.

This situation was unusual, but it did happen on rare occasions. The unlearned skills were a lost opportunity; and the joys of accomplishment were lost. The parent was unsuccessful in working through this situation with her daughter and made excuses for her rather than helping her overcome her stubborn resistance, a problem that would return and grow if not handled. Her daughter needed to do that paper for many reasons, the most important being that you need to do things that you don't want to do. You need to be obedient and you need to be respectful of authority. I felt sorry and defeated in this situation. I felt like I had failed this student by letting her and her mother fail themselves.

Many cultural backgrounds exist that can cause students to stand out in negative ways. Vincent was one of those students. Why, asked the teachers, did his father tie his shoes and feed him cereal in the morning. Obviously, Vincent was spoiled and pampered, which contributed to his disrespectful attitude toward his classmates and female teachers. Vincent was an exceptionally bright gifted student, and he knew it. His intellect shone like the noontide sun on a clear day. His sense of superiority bred an inner restlessness. He delighted in attention-getting antics. The girls grew tired of being pinched, and the boys resented the ways their pencils and papers disappeared or landed on the floor in a remote corner of the classroom.

Vincent was tall for a third grader. He was built like a well-fed bull that had spent his days dreaming in a soft bed of shaded green grass, which put him at a great disadvantage on the physical education field. Rose colored cheeks blended into his ivory smooth complexion. Trimmed closely to his head, thick black hair highlighted the charcoal eyes that danced with a teasing grin whenever he was caught in wrongdoing.

His mother was an American-born citizen and taught Spanish in a nearby high school. His dad was employed by a small company near their home.

Vincent had an older sister, Rachel, who bordered on perfection. Excellent grades were the result of her conscientious work ethic. She didn't look down on her brother, but she tried to distance herself from him, especially whenever he got into trouble. She made it clear that his behavior had nothing to do with her. She didn't want to be identified with any of his problems.

During the early years, when I taught both Vincent and his sister, their mother made it a point to come to the scheduled conferences. When the conversation focused on Vincent, she became uncomfortably defensive. After Rachel went on to middle school, Vincent's mother seldom came to visit. It was Vincent's father who signed the yearly educational plan, allowing his son to take part in the gifted program the following year.

Vincent's father treated him like a royal prince, which concerned many of his teachers. They didn't understand why his parents enabled and encouraged his superior attitude. Vincent saw the world through a self-centered ego. He had grown up to expect others to serve his every need, which included tying his shoes. The teachers believed this indulgence hindered Vincent's brilliant mind, which had so much potential.

Challenged by his constant disruptions, I spent many long nights searching for positive ways to develop his talents and relationships with others.

He loved sharing his knowledge with the class, so I often gave him the opportunity to express himself and feel important. This improved his behavior.

He shared information about many of the books that were his constant companions. The planets and their satellites were of great interest to him. He knew about the Oort Cloud and was fascinated with black holes.

I later learned that Vincent's father came from a small city in Northeast Iran, where men were considered superior to women and were treated accordingly. This went a long way in explaining Vincent's elite, disdainful attitude.

One day Vincent mentioned that his grandmother was going to visit from Iran. Since I was interested in any resource that could enrich the experiences of my students, I asked Vincent if his grandmother would like to visit our classroom. A crafty glimmer spread across his face. The thought of having his grandmother visit our classroom lit up his expression like sparklers going off on the Fourth of July. Although he remained silent, his eyes gleamed with anticipation.

I was unaware of the circumstances I had set into motion with this request. I had envisioned a woman walking into our classroom and telling the students about Iran. If we were lucky, she might have some pictures or items to share. This was an opportunity for Vincent to give the class some knowledge of his cultural background and to feel some positive attention from his classmates. I was unprepared for what was about to take place.

Vincent's father walked his mother from the car into the classroom. She clung to his arm for guidance and security. She did not wear any makeup and I immediately saw the family resemblance. The breeze blew her long robe and scarf into billowing clouds of black. It startled all my expectations. Never had I been so close to someone dressed like this. She brought me face to face with a strange, unfamiliar moment in time. She was not a dream. She was real and in my classroom. I couldn't just stare at her. She came because I had invited her. She was my guest. My first responsibility was to make her feel comfortable. I put my feelings aside.

Immediately I went over to meet her. I offered her a chair. I wonder what she was feeling. She couldn't speak or understand our language; she couldn't read any of the signs or words. Our alphabet was totally incomprehensible. Cars, lights, buildings, and a complicated environment of technology were all unfamiliar. Children and adults were dressed in shorts and tank tops. Girls and boys shared the same classroom. The small remote village in the mountains of Iran must have felt far away to her.

Yet this foreign land encompassed her son's life. He had a family and a way of life that separated the two of them not only in miles, but also in ideals and culture.

I looked into her dark, deep set eyes with a welcoming smile. Suddenly her hands grasped my shoulders and pulled me close to her. She kissed both of my cheeks with heartfelt emotion. She was enveloped in a black robe; I was wearing a tan pant suit. She was Muslim; I was Christian. We had no way of talking with each other. We were total strangers, yet I felt a warm, all-embracing love and rejoiced in the connection I experienced. I was overwhelmed and will never forget that moment.

How could I feel so strongly and with such compassion for someone I had never met? Our homes were on opposite sides of the ocean, yet our hearts knew each other. Why did she care so much and why did I respond so deeply? It made me realize that there truly is a oneness of spirit that has nothing to do with material circumstances.

I was concerned about making Vincent's grandmother feel at home with the students. Vincent's father waved away my worries. His mother just wanted to sit and watch, and that is what she did until he picked her up at lunchtime. I put my arms around her and gave her a hug. She disappeared from our lives, but she left an impression that will be with me forever.

I looked at Vincent in a different way after her visit. Somehow, I loved him more. I felt a greater tolerance for his attitude. He also responded to me with an enhanced degree of respect.

The following year, I asked Vincent how his grandmother was doing. He hesitated for a moment—first looking down at the floor, then looking up and staring into my eyes. He solemnly told me she had died. His eyes searched mine, looking for my reaction. I told Vincent I was sorry, that he had a very special grandmother, and that he should always treasure the time they had spent together.

I felt privileged and humbled to have met her and hoped she had felt touched by the same love she had given to me.

I look out over the ocean and watch the glow of a sunset filling the sky. Vibrant shades of pink and scarlet burst forth in a life that radiates a splendor no one can invent or buy. It comes to every blade of grass, to every flower and to every man, woman and child. It is there for the rich and the poor, for the busiest cities, the smallest mud huts hidden in the rainforest of Africa or in the villages scattered among the majestic Himalayan Mountains in Asia. We share the sun's light. It belongs to us all. That understanding made all the difference.

CHAPTER 6

THE STRUGGLE TO BE PERFECT

Gifted students are expected to excel in school. They are respected, admired, and looked up to as leaders. It is assumed that no one with such a high IQ makes mistakes or struggles with assignments. The label of gifted puts a lot of added pressure on a child who has already felt isolated in a bubble of perfection. Anything that would challenge their reputation could suspend them in a foreign terrain and cause a great deal of anxiety. The positive self-image that feeds their confidence level is based on the success they have experienced when they were little or their ability to perform above other children their age.

Living up to this kind of reputation emboldens some students. They shine in many positive ways. For some, however, the whole scenario cascades into stress. Coping with the idea that you are gifted creates an inner fear that is not fun. Students feel obligated to maintain an elevated image, which provides them with admiration and esteem. Relinquishing the respect that had become the fountain for their feelings of self-worth would be devastating. Being perfect was not a choice, it was an obligation they had to maintain for their teachers, friends, parents, family, and most of all for themselves. They couldn't make a mistake. It would be far easier to just give up than to try and fail.

Excuses were quick to come when an assignment seemed difficult. I heard such things as "my head hurts," "I feel sick," "it's too hard," "would you do it for me?" "Can we work with someone else?" "Can I take this home to finish?" Sometimes a student would break down in tears. One example was a young boy who was shy and soft spoken. He did not put much effort into his work and often did not complete the assignments. His mother was a teacher and had a strong, sweet mothering quality that protected her son like a swan whose wings covered her young with calm protective might. Jonathan was a perfect son —obedient, well-mannered, and accustomed to being sheltered from discomfort of any kind.

One afternoon I received a note requesting that Jonathan be removed from the gifted class. It was too difficult for him, the note read. As I read the words, I felt my thoughts rebel. I knew the work wasn't too hard; it was challenging, and Jonathan felt defeated by its expectations. He had never faced something that required work beyond his comfort zone so he wanted to quit. In order to make her son happy, his mother was willing to accommodate his wishes.

After a long conversation with the mother, where I firmly disagreed with her request, it was decided to keep him in the program. Now Jonathan had to face his responsibilities or risk failure, something he had never dealt with before, the fear of not being perfect. Jonathan turned out to be one of my strongest students. The qualities he developed in the gifted program prepared him to conquer new challenges in the future.

Sometimes it takes strength, faith, and trust; but it is worth every sulking tear and anguished decision. I have often had to remind myself that nothing is perfect, but everything is possible. Knowing the importance of working through what I call a perfection disorder, I was on a constant outlook for opportunities to help my students overcome their self-limiting outcomes. I knew I needed to be stern and firm as well as encouraging. I couldn't sympathize with their self-defeating attitudes by giving into the tears and making everything easy for them. My mission was to strengthen their resolve and free them from their insecurity and self-doubts. They needed to accept themselves without feeling they had to be perfect. It was their battle to fight, and victory would bring them the joy of self-fulfillment. For some students, the battle was defensive and belligerent, but the outcome was far more important than the struggle it took to achieve its rewards. I did not want to deprive these students of the lessons they needed to learn in order to develop the success they were so capable of obtaining.

Comparing these gifted students with their peers was enlightening. They were not in the top reading group, their writing was sloppy, and math was too difficult to get a perfect paper. Most of all, nothing they did was perfect or easy. Some of these students grew to believe more in themselves than the gifted students did. They had developed a mental muscle that came from such qualities as tenacity, perseverance, devotion, and pushing to succeed despite a history of mistakes and poor grades. In many ways, their determination enabled them to achieve beyond the gifted student, who never had the need to develop these qualities. Many of these students did better in school than their gifted counterparts. What my gifted students needed was confidence in themselves coupled with an inner strength and courage. I wanted them to discover their inner worth, which was not dependent on their image of perfection.

From the time a gifted child could remember, they were admired and their parents bragged about them to their friends. They grew up feeling proud of their quick brightness. It had become something they had learned about themselves, and they knew it was good. It was what they leaned on for acceptance. It made them feel that attention and praise came from their ability, everyone expected them to be perfect, and at their young age perfection was effortless. But as the years went by, they were put into circumstances that made them question their own ability to be perfect all the time. This challenged their confidence. What would people think of them if they made a mistake and their friends found out they weren't perfect after all? Would they still be friends? Would people still like them? Would their teachers still think they were smart? And if they didn't what would happen? It felt like life depended on their ability to perform perfectly, and without this ability, their whole world would crumble in failure. They were like water balloons being tossed over a bed of nails.

We can help these children by challenging them at an early age. They need to be put in situations that help them stretch and experience opportunities that result in mistakes that build into successful outcomes. We need to let them see us make mistakes and learn from them, letting them know we do not give up or get downgraded because things did not go perfectly. It is essential that we not worship a gifted child, treating them as if they are better than other children. We do not want to make their world problem-free. Children should not be sheltered from challenging situations. We need to let them know that they are loved unconditionally because they are innately good, not because they have a high IQ or because you think they are perfect. It is okay to make mistakes; they are learning tools. They are not signs of weakness or failure.

A happy, well-lived life is spent with humility and unselfish love. No matter how gifted a child may be, their real source of happiness will be found in what they give to others not in feeling superior in doing things faster than others. If I were to give a parent of a gifted child advice, I would tell them not to focus on their child's IQ, but instead, help them care for other people. Inspire them to strive to do their best, but not because they are better than others, but because they have been given a gift; and a gift is for giving.

Thomas Edison tried thousands of times before he invented the light bulb. That meant he made thousands of mistakes. Edison understood that each mistake was another step closer to inventing a light bulb successfully. He never gave up. We are not educating gifted children to feel better than others, we are bringing up the future, which needs our quickest learners to be free to experiment, to try without quitting and to believe in themselves without fearing failure.

Gifted students need to love who they are; not because they are perfect, but because they can contribute to helping their world. They need to accept all people of all abilities and walks of life. No matter what the IQ score, there is a gift in us all. We need each other, and we need to be grateful for every little or big thing that has contributed to making our world better for all mankind. That is perfection at its very best.

CHAPTER 7

ENCOURAGEMENT

"**I**t's not my mess why should I have to clean it up?"

"That's what the book said, I just copied it. I have no idea what it means." "It's too hard."

"I didn't do it because my mother had a meeting and she wasn't home to do it. It's her fault."

These are a few of the most common excuses that swelled through the gifted classes and were a daily occurrence. Occasionally I heard something more original like "my dog ate my homework" or "my milk spilled all over it and my dad threw it in the garbage." Excuses swelled through the gifted classroom like ocean tides in the bay of Funday. They tamped down the progress and learning capacity of my students. Something had to be done to avoid turning myself into an ogre with dictator tendencies, which would destroy the positive learning environment. I searched the repertoire of my credible solutions for an answer. I wanted my students to develop a responsible, self-directed honest approach to their work and to discover the joy in doing so.

I remembered a favorite comic strip in a magazine that my children read when they were younger. It was about two very different personalities. Goofy was always doing things that got him into trouble. While Gallant was a shining example of good behavior and thoughtfulness. I decided on using Gallant as the example for a more positive attitude. Goofy was too negative, so I came up with two generic names, Pat and Sal. Pat would represent the scattered unorganized forgetful student, and Sal was the student who was satisfied with just getting by and depended on others to organize his time and take responsibility for helping him get his work done on time.

I got some construction paper, cut out three characters and put them on the wall. Pat was sloppy and barely holding together. His facial expression resembled a spaced-out child that looked lost and unorganized. Sal was put together but looked average. There was nothing exceptional or special about him. His expression was not happy or sad. Gallant, however, was smiling with confidence and pride. He was immaculately dressed with many extra additions to his attire. Gallant had an aura of satisfaction and confidence. These three characters became examples of the varying attitudes of my students and would help serve as reminders for my class. The characters would help them reflect on their own behaviors in simple, lighthearted ways.

I had a list of character traits that each of these three personalities expressed. The qualities were posted on the wall next to their owner and were often referred to when needed. They illustrated the outcomes of the choices the children made as they were building toward a successful future, which they all wanted.

I let the class know that each one of them was a Gallant. But if any took the path of Pat or Sal, life would not provide them with the positive recognition they all wanted. Everyone was capable if they were willing to put forth the effort to do their best, and I was there to help in any way I could. Gallant became the standard bearer for the excellence, and I expected every student to adhere.

PAT'S PERSONALITY:

He forgets his homework.
His papers are unorganized.
He doesn't clean up his mess.
He doesn't want to help others.
He loses his notes and permission slips.
He doesn't have pencils or paper.

He gives up.
He gets bored.
He fools around.
He hates to lose.
He doesn't believe in himself.

SAL'S PERSONALITY:
He expects the parent to tell him to do homework.
He does only what he has to do.
He only cleans up his own mess.
He doesn't do extra things.
He does not try too hard.
He would rather fool around than get his work done.
He doesn't like to lose.
He thinks he is better than others.
He doesn't listen to others.

GALLANT'S PERSONALITY:
He does his homework without parents telling him.
He does his best.
He stays on track.
He cleans up his mess and the room even if it isn't his mess
He does more than he is asked.
He helps others.
He brings supplies.
He doesn't give up.
He's a good sport.
He believes in himself.
He listens to others.
He shares his ideas.

At the beginning of each year, I sent home a welcoming letter with a request for specific items. We needed Oreo cookies, Cool Whip, M&Ms, assorted candies, plates, plastic spoons, and sprinkles. We put them aside until after lunch. With the class watching, I opened a package of Oreo cookies and took one out, purposefully dropping it on the floor and stepping on it slightly. After picking up the obviously dirty and damaged Oreo, I asked if anyone wanted it. The class moaned in disgust. I then took a fresh cookie out of the package and placed it on a plate explaining that it was an average everyday cookie. Everyone liked it; it was good. We all agreed. Meanwhile the class was excited, and their appetites were increasing at a rapid rate. Then I held up the third cookie and topped it with Cool Whip and sprinkles and then asked the class to choose which of the three cookies they would like best. They all wanted the Oreo with the Cool Whip and sprinkles, of course.

A perfect opportunity to go over the three different kinds of students the cookies represented: Pat who was unorganized and messy, Sal who was plain and uninterested in doing anything or didn't have to, or Gallant who was so much more and did his best.

The class clearly got the message and were all anxious to make their own Gallant Oreo cookie creation. We passed out plates, spoons, cookies, Cool Whip, M&Ms, and sprinkles to each table and watched the magic happen. Amazing things materialized; we had castles, trucks, abstract designs, and an incredible variety of Gallant Oreos. Everyone had a great time and enjoyed sharing their ideas with the class. After we devoured our creations, I went to the wall where Pat, Sal, and Gallant were waiting.

This activity was a great way to introduce the attitudes I expected to see during the year. When I heard the commonly used excuses for lost papers, I would look to the wall and to Gallant and remind my students that Gallant was dependable and responsible. He never misplaced his homework, losing homework was not a Gallant thing to do. If I was looking through a notebook with pages sticking out and with writing that was sloppy, I didn't need to reprimand the student. This process didn't work 100 percent of the time, but helped lay a foundation for excellence on the children's minds. Pat, Sal, and Gallant served us well.

CHAPTER 8

GIFTS FOR THE TEACHER

Sitting in a classroom with my teacher whose desk was over flowing with beautiful wrapped gifts made me feel embarrassed and guilty. None of those colorful offerings belonged to me. Remembering the excitement, the oohs and aahs that filled the room as my class watched each gift as it was unwrapped, brought back unhappy memories. Barbie Brown's mother had a kiln in her basement, and her mother always made an artistic ceramic dish we all admired, each one especially made for a teacher. Sandy Koss always brought something that looked like it could have been showcased in a department store window. It was always a contest to see whose gift was the nicest and most expensive. The presents that were small were the ones we all looked upon with disdain. Worse yet were the students who didn't even bring a gift for their teacher at Christmas time. It made me feel like I didn't care. Would my teacher like the kids that brought gifts more than me? I wondered about that sometimes. I don't know why I never asked my mother to buy a gift so I could also feel proud.

My mother wasn't ungrateful, she just was too busy being a mother of five children and never thought about buying a present for the teachers. It was a little thing, not anything that plagued me until I was a teacher, and the lovely gifts started filling my desk with anxious children anticipating the joy they would experience when I opened their gift.

That's when it kicked in. At first, I didn't understand the overwhelming feeling that kept me from opening any presents in front of the class; I certainly didn't want to disappoint anyone. I tried to analyze my attitude as it all came back. The self-conscious embarrassment, the comparing of gifts and their value. I couldn't open the gifts in front of the class, I just couldn't. I thought of all the students who did not bring a present, and I did not want them to feel the way I did as a child. I explained that if they wanted me to open their gift they could come before school started in the morning or after school in the afternoon; many of them did just that. It was an issue that surfaced every year with my students. Explaining that I did not want to make anyone uncomfortable wasn't easily understood by everyone. But the memories that kept me from opening gifts in front of the class clung to my consciousness like overcooked macaroni sticking to the bottom of a pan. It wasn't a choice; it was a reality.

Through the years I received many wonderful gifts, which gave me a grateful understanding that I was appreciated. Those gifts meant a lot to me and validated my place and success with the families. I was privileged to serve. Gifts mean a lot to teachers, and I was thankful for each one of them.

INTRUDUCTION TO CURRICULUM

During the years that I taught the gifted program, we studied a variety of subjects. Some were more successful and popular than others. I have written about some of the best ones. These ideas worked well. This is not a how-to book, but the activities and concepts will provide you with ideas you might want to use. If you are a teacher, home school parent, or group leader of any kind, you will find the projects and goals to be inspiring and extremely helpful. You may be able to use the internet to research more deeply the subjects that interest you. That is the purpose of these starting points. I hope they open doors with new ideas and lead you on adventures you never imagined possible. Learning is an avenue that opens minds and leads to self-discovery. It is a world of excitement and joy with no end in sight. I'm so grateful to share these beginnings with you.

TOPICS OF UDY

Deciding on the subject to study each year is up to each individual teacher in Florida. Today there are lessons already written out along with goals and activities. The topic that is chosen is only a gateway to a wide, wonderful pathway of experiences your students are about to take part in. The freedom to formulate a curriculum is unequalled in the regular classroom. For anyone who is creative and enjoys charting their own territory, teaching the gifted class is a dream come true. I was able to put myself into what I taught. The most important things I wanted to convey to my students went beyond the learning. I wanted my students to enjoy the pursuit of knowledge. I also felt it was important to expand their view of the world and its problems, values and beauty.

I wanted them to have an open, accepting mind and to develop a thirst to know more and to care for others in the process.

The gifted students needed to learn how to discipline themselves and to be willing to strive for excellence. Expecting the best from themselves helped them to reject attitudes of apathy or being satisfied with just the minimum effort. My goal was to use my chosen topic as the way to help them grow intellectually and morally. I was an example, so I needed to find subjects that were exciting to me. The topics needed to touch on many different facets of life in order to provide my classes with a wide variety of learning experiences during the five years they would be in elementary school. Below you'll find a list of the subjects I chose. I never got tired or bored with the learning opportunities they provided. I have included a summary of each. There is a more detailed rendition in later pages.

<u>Art</u> – the history of European Art. This unit covered all periods from Cave art through Contemporary art of today. It showed the way art expressed the life and attitudes of the times and included music and history.

<u>World Geography</u> – discussed the formation of earth. This unit covered the seven continents and problems facing our world. It helped students understand diversity and varying perspectives of all people.

<u>Space</u> – worked to ignite our imagination and knowledge of our solar system and universe.

<u>Animal Life</u> – concentrated on our environment and the fascinating life of insects, microscopic animals, and endangered species.

<u>Communications and Inventions</u> - studied the qualities of famous people, inventors, and inventions.

<u>Economic</u> – this was for fifth grade. The students produced and sold a product.

<u>Manners</u> – a short study of etiquette and table manners.

<u>Oceans</u> – a year of studying our oceans, the life that we know and never knew about, sharks, whales, and pollution. The topics were coupled with animal life.

<u>Writing</u> – encouraged self-expression. This unit gave students the opportunity to explore and interpret the world around them.

<u>1800s</u> - To inspire students to appreciate the history of our country. Students learned to think about other people and the way they thought and lived 150 years ago.

Teaching was like a mission to me. I wanted to inspire an appreciation and compassion for other people and all living things without regard to skin color, nationality, greed or varying life styles. This kind of learning is far more important than IQ or test scores. It opens hearts and ends prejudice. It can insure that our children can grow up with dreams and a safe future; it can save our world.

CHAPTER 9

SPACE

MAIN OBJEIVE

This unit explores the universe(s), inspires the imagination, and teaches about our possibilities for living in space. It is for dreamers and scientists alike. Many grades include the planets in their science curriculum. But few, if any, take up the study of satellites, the Oort Cloud, infinity, black holes, worm holes, or the possibility of several universes. There is so much more to study and embrace when studying space. It is exciting and mind-opening.

We learned how space exploration has made earth a better place to live. We expanded our mental horizons to the infinite universes beyond our present understanding. How is it possible to live in outer space? What would it be like to find life on another planet? What would a life be like in order to survive on any one of the other planets or satellites? Looking at the problems we face in the future, can we discover answers in outer space?

Astronauts are sometimes available to come to your school. Cape Kennedy has some very informative lessons and information that you can send away for. A good way to approach this unit is to have the students think about looking for alternative places to live other than earth. Some questions to ask are: What would you need to survive?

What would you have to wear? What would you eat? Design a space suit – what do you need to live? Design a space ship – what would you need? Halloween night on the planets. What kind of life forms could survive on satellites and planets?

SUCCESSFUL ACTIVITIES

1) Design a spaceship and suit.

2) Design an amusement park using the planets as rides.

3) Invent a living being that could survive on each planet. How would such beings breathe? What would they eat? Etc.

4) Quiz Bowl

5) What would you find on the other side of a worm hole or black hole?

6) What things would you like to learn about space?

7) Keep a chart comparing planets and satellites.

8) Purchase rocket kits and launch them in an open area.

EXTRA MATERIALS

1) Write to Kennedy Space Center for materials.

2) Local library has many books to give ideas and important information.

FIELD TRIP

1) Kennedy Space Center.

2) Science museum with a planetarium.

TREASURE HUNT

The year is 3000 AD. The earth is overpopulated. Food and water are scarce. You have just returned from a trip from the planets. It has been a wonderful adventure that lasted 25 years. A lot has happened on earth. Presidents have come and gone. Children have grown into adults who have children of their own. Your space ship is loaded with artifacts that you have collected, along with some amazing photographs. Everyone is anxious to see what you have. Your team carefully arranges everything in a special museum that you will now create. Did you find a place for humans to live?

1) The first planet is Mars. It has two satellites: ______________ (Deimos) and ______________ (Phobos). Draw a picture of them and tell which is bigger. Could we live on Mars? How?

2) The asteroid belt was difficult to pass through. You managed to collect stones from this part of our planetary system. Show us these artifacts and tell how you got them. Put your story on a piece of paper.

3) Once you were out in space and free from the asteroid belt, you began to see the satellites around Jupiter. Name six of the satellites and color them, telling something you discovered about each one. Could we live on one of the satellites?

4) When you see the beautiful rings around Saturn and its many satellites, the artist in you comes alive. Draw what you see. Could we live there? How?

5) The farther we go from earth, the farther we are from the sun. It is dark. How cold is it on Neptune? Could we live there? How? Or why not?

6) The next planet is different from all the others because ______________ (Uranus rotates counter-clockwise).

7) You know Pluto is no longer a planet. Why did it lose its title of "planet"? Write and sing a song about Pluto and how it must feel to be left out of our planets to the tune of "Twinkle, Twinkle Little Star." The song must be at least ten lines long, and your whole group must sing it together.

8) You didn't go out in space past Uranus because it was too dark and cold, and you were afraid you would run out of fuel. You therefore missed seeing the ______________(Oort) cloud.

9) The clothes and items you took are all messed up. Help straighten them up. Unscramble the letters: shirt, space suit, oxygen, gloves.

10) You get bored in space. There isn't much to do. Invent a musical instrument you can play to pass the time.

11) Before you can return to earth, you have to visit the two planets that are closer to the sun than Earth. They are ______________(Mercury) and ___________________(Venus).

12) Which planet is the hottest? Why?

QUIZ BOWL

Here are some suggestions for the quiz bowl:

1) Name the planets.

2) Which planet is the hottest?

3) Name a constellation.

4) What keeps Venus from ever cooling down?

5) What are the two moons or satellites orbiting Mars?

6) Is there a possibility that there is more than one universe?

7) How many satellites are orbiting Saturn? (A. 10, B. 1, C. 15 or more)

8) What are the rings around Saturn made of?

9) What is the huge red spot on Jupiter?

10) Which satellites have active volcanos?

11) Why isn't Pluto a planet anymore?

12) Where and what is the Oort Cloud?

13) What is a red giant?

14) What is a white dwarf?

15) How old do we think earth is?

16) Scientists guess that there are how many galaxies? (A. 2 million B. 2 billion C. 1 trillion)

17) How can it be colder on Mars than on earth?

18) Which is the hottest star? Red star, white star, or blue star?

19) What is a black hole?

20) What is a super nova?

21) Do we have a black hole in our solar system?

22) We have amazing pictures from space from the _______________ (Hubble telescope).

23) How many stars are out there?

24) What is the Big Bang Theory?

25) We had a space race with another country called ___________
(Russia).

26) What is a comet?

27) What was the first living thing to go into space?

28) What is Sputnik?

29) What is a worm hole?

30) Name someone who walked on the moon. Scientists have discovered that some of the dust particles on the moon could be from earth. How could this be?

31) When you see the light from a star, it could be dead and no longer there. How could this be?

32) How fast does light travel? What is a lightyear?

33) When you see people floating in a spaceship, it is because

____

34) What color is the sky in space? Are the days and nights longer and shorter on different planets? Why?

35) What do you call the time it takes for a planet to go around the sun?

RESEARCH TOPICS

1) Are we alone in the universe?

2) Research global warming. Do you think it is true? If so, how can we stop it? If not, why do people think it is true?

3) Research the life of one of the astronauts. Would you like to be an astronaut? What would you have to do to become an astronaut?

4) Research one of our space missions. Where did the mission go and what did it discover? What future mission would you like to see? (Clementine, Magellan, Neveras, Stardust, Luna, Galileo, Lunik, Cassini, Pluto Express, Sputnik are some space missions to choose from.)

5) Research the Hubble Telescope and some pictures that it took. Tell us what you have learned from these pictures. Should we abandon the telescope? What would take its place?

6) Research the decision that Pluto is no longer considered part of our solar system. Should it have been done? Why or why not?

7) Research the early astronomers such as Galileo, Aristotle, Herschel, Newton, and Copernicus. What did they discover and what did they think that was later proven wrong? Mistakes happen. What do you think about someone being so smart and yet making mistakes?

8) Research space robots. How have they helped us in our space exploration? How could we use them in the future for learning about space?

9) Research our moon. Do you think we could ever live on the moon? How could that happen? Would you like to live on the moon? Why?

10) Research the space station. How do the astronauts live? What problems did the space station have? Would you like to live in space? Why?

11) Research the race to the moon between the United States and the Soviet Union. Who do you think will be the first to land on Mars? Why?

12) Make a report of careers having to do with space. Choose two that you would like and two that you would not like and tell why.

13) Research pollution on earth. Give some solutions to the problems we have with fossil fuels or other pollution problems on earth.

14) Research time travel. Can we go back in time or forward into the future?

15) Research different galaxies and how to identify them by their shape.

16) Research ways that space exploration can help our planet. What have we learned from space that makes our everyday life better now and in the future?

17) Research the theory that the earth was hit by an asteroid and made the dinosaurs disappear. Do you agree or disagree?

Getting ready to launch on rocket day

CREATIVE PROJECTS

1) Create an amusement park with a space theme.

2) Create a board game with a space theme.

3) Make a robot for space exploration. Explain where your robot would go and what it would do. (If you have done a robot in the past do not choose this one again)

4) Make up a story about space travel.

5) Write a poem about each of the planets. Keep in mind the Greek and Roman name for each planet.

6) Create a model of a space station. Remember to include food, sleeping places, exercise rooms, etc.

7) Draw a series of pictures showing the birth of a planet and explain it to the class.

8) Make a dictionary about space with at least 35 terms. Illustrate your book.

9) Create a solar system newspaper with news from every planet. Be sure to include a gossip column, headlines, funnies, puzzles, and current events.

10) Do you believe in aliens? Find research to support your opinion. Make drawings of at least three different aliens and tell how they are different from us.

11) You have discovered an alien dictionary. What would you find in the book that would make it different from ours? Include 26 words in your dictionary.

12) Create a suitcase that you would take to a specific place in the universe outside of our solar system. Include objects, stories, newspaper articles, dolls, stamps, pictures, etc.

13) Create a museum of space objects that stands in the center of our galaxy. What would it look like and what things would you put in it?

14) Select two pieces of music inspired by space. Make three pieces of sculpture or drawings of what the composer wanted you to see or feel from his music. Examples: *Star Wars*, *Star Trek*, *The Planets* by Gustav Holtz.

15) Create three paintings of the universe in two different styles of art. Example: Impressionism, Abstractionism.

16) Create a planet that could exist somewhere in space. Make a model including people, climate, and houses.

- 61 -

CHAPTER 10

HISTORY OF EUROPEAN ART

MAIN OBJECTIVE

This unit helps students to appreciate Art, to create different expressions of themselves and to see how art and music reflect the time in history during which they were created.

SUCCESSFUL ACTIVITIES

1) Make a self-portrait sculpture with a Styrofoam wig head

2) Make a color wheel

3) Paint a landscape painting with acrylic paint

4) Experiment with primary colors and white clay to make different colors

5) Record music from different historical periods match with its art

6) Join Creative Connections

GUEST SPEAKER

Visual artist speaker from local museum

FIELD TRIPS

Art museum, musical concert, Renaissance festival

EXTRA MATERIAL

Acrylic paints, plaster rolls, old sheets, pillow cases, old shirts, Styrofoam heads ordered in bulk from a wig shop, brushes, canvas

This year, we started with cave art and went through Medieval, Renaissance, Classical, Romanticism, Impressionism, Post-Impressionism, Surrealism, Abstract, Abstract-Expressionism, and studied specific artists. As we studied each movement, we also studied the times and history that helped produce the art, since the art work reflected the times in which they were created. Music also expresses the world. It was interesting to connect art with music and understand how interrelated they were in mood and subject matter.

One familiar project that the class enjoyed was taping paper on the bottom of each desk and having the students lie on their backs to draw a picture as Michelangelo did with the Sistine Chapel. Contacting nearby art museums for field trips is a natural outcome of this year. It would be great to ask if they have any floating exhibits available. They may also have volunteer speakers who will come to your school and talk about specific art subjects. There are so many topics to study with this unit. Be careful to organize your time so that you can cover what is most important to you. This was the year that enabled me to communicate my love of art to my students. It was an exciting year. My main objective was to teach my students the importance of art and its beauty. I wanted them to learn how to express themselves and how to understand others through art.

Some of the best projects in this unit were covering a Styrofoam head (ordered from a wig shop) with strips of plaster to make a self-portrait.

Once the heads were sculpted to resemble hair style and facial features, we painted them and added any details each child desired. We also had each child purchase a stretched canvas – I ordered acrylic paint from the warehouse, with necessary brushes. We covered chairs with old pillow cases and went outside to paint preplanned landscape pictures. I put paint on Styrofoam plates for each child. Everyone had a paper cup of water and paper towels. It took about a month to complete the paintings. We started with the background first, and then used white chalk to sketch trees, etc. It was fun being outside and watching the pictures take shape based on lessons that had led up to this point.

QUIZ BOWL QUESTIONS

These questions were based on the things I stressed. I will give you some samples.

1) Who painted the Mona Lisa?

2) What is a fresco?

3) What makes medieval art different from Renaissance art?

4) Name a famous artist from the Renaissance.

5) What was *The Last Supper* about?

6) During what period were the cathedrals built?

7) Name something the Impressionists loved.

8) What is a bust?

9) Who painted the ceiling of the Sistine Chapel?

10) What was Rembrandt famous for?

11) What was pointillism?

12) Name the primary colors.

13) What color comes from mixing yellow and blue?

14) How would you make pink?

15) What is a canvas?

16) Who painted *Water Lilies*?

17) What is abstract expressionism?

18) What is perspective?

19) What is a horizon line?

20) What is a vanishing point?

21) Who painted *The Potato Eaters*?

22) How many paintings did Van Gogh sell before he died?

23) Tell something you remember about Picasso.

24) Why did Picasso paint *Guernica*?

25) Who was famous for Surrealism?

26) Name a surreal painting and state what it was about.

27) What is something that makes a piece of art great?

CREATIVE CONNECTIONS

This organization is an excellent one. They work with schools all over the world to help children understand other cultures and to share their own ideas and customs. They are located in California. Contact them at 916-566-1870.

1) The first thing that will happen is you will choose the country you are most interested in.

2) You will be assigned a school to communicate with.

3) You will have a class fill out information about themselves, and then mail it to the school in that country.

4) Your partner class will also fill out information and send it to you.

5) Each student in your class will decide on a favorite activity and make a picture, putting in details and writing their names on the back explaining what it is about. The pictures can be paintings, chalk, crayons, collages, or a combination.

6) You send the pictures to your partner school; they do the same. It is very exciting to receive the pictures and look at them. You discover so many different things and connect with children that in many ways are very much the same, even though they live in a different part of the world.

7) If children in the partner school do not speak English, Creative Connections will translate for you.

8) This can be done for any subject – not just art. I did it for geography, as well.

9) The pictures are posted on the internet and feature work by the creating class.

TREASURE HUNT

It is a beautiful world, and Alice and Isaiah love living in it. They have so much love for their world they have decided to create a museum dedicated to beautiful things and to artists who brought this beauty to our attention in different ways. Your job is to collect things for the museum and display them for others to see. (Use a box for your museum.)

1) To collect art you must understand color. Make a color wheel including primary and secondary colors. Use play dough, crayons, chalk.

2) Every artist finds some inspiration from nature. Find something from nature for your museum.

3) You have discovered two very old paintings in the basement of an antique shop in St. Petersburg. After wiping off the dust, you can see that one painting is from medieval times and one is from the Renaissance. Draw both paintings and be able to tell which is from 1000 and which is from 1570. What makes them different?

4) Name a famous artist from the classical period and explain two things that help you know the classical period.

5) Draw a picture of Monet in his later years.

6) Explain what made the Impressionist movement. What was it all about?

7) Picasso was sad for a period in his life. What did he do to tell you how sad he felt?

8) Who painted the *Potato Eaters*? Why did the artist paint such a dark picture?

9) Rembrandt loved to paint with a hidden source of light in his paintings. Draw a picture that Rembrandt would like to call his own.

10) You are going outside to paint. What things will you need? Scramble the following words for students to unscramble: painting shirt, paintbrushes, canvas, paint, water, inspiration.

11) Put together a still life using things that are less than two inches in size.

12) Making pictures look three dimensional is not easy unless you know the art of ___________(perspective).

13) Draw a picture using this technique.

14) His wife was Gala. Who was he? What did he call his art style?

15) Write a song eight lines long that rhymes and can be sung to the tune "You are my Sunshine." The song can be about anything we learned in art this year.

16) Name a new art movement that will represent our life today. What will make it tell about the way people live and think today?

RESEARCH REPORT

1) Research cave art and drawings. Tell what they mean about the life of the cave dwellers. Do you think they were happy?

2) Research the architecture of Europe during the Medieval – Renaissance periods. How can you tell the difference between those two periods? Which do you like better?

3) Research the cathedrals. How were they built and why?

4) Research the times between Medieval and Renaissance. What brought on the Renaissance, and how did the art change in the Renaissance? What do you like best? Why?

5) Write about a famous artist. Tell how his life influenced his paintings. Do you like his early or later work? Why?

6) Research the kings and queens in Europe. Tell how they influenced art and music. Do you think this was good or not so good?

7) Art and music are a lot alike. They reflect the time in which they were created. Pick a period of art and compare the art and music that was created during that time. How do they tell you about the people and how they lived?

8) Dali was very creative. Research one of his paintings and tell about its meaning. Do you like it?

9) Research and report on cave men art. Do one of the following: (a) tell what it teaches us about the way they lived; or (b) compare it with modern day art and tell why you think it is different. An example would be how they drew people and animals compared to the way they are drawn today.

10) Research paint and how it is made, and how it has changed over the years. Do you think it has improved?

11) What do you think of abstract art? Research an artist who is an abstract artist. Do you like it? Why?

12) Is art important for world peace? Why or why not? Give examples.

13) Research and report on ancient Egyptian art and do one of the following: (a) tell what their art communicates about the way the ancient Egyptians lived; (b) connect their lifestyle to Rome and Greece; or (c) research mummies and pyramids.

14) Pick a period and country from Asia and research its art. Tell why you think it has its own individual style.

15) Research and report on a country in Africa and a period of its history. What are some styles or ideas that you see in this art? Does it tell you anything about the artist and the way the people lived in that country?

16) Research and report on different styles of architecture. Pick one that you like and tell why. Example: Romanesque, Classical, Rococo, and Baroque.

17) Research and report on musical instruments, their countries origin, and what they tell us about the people that played them. Example: Where did the piano originate? Has it changed at all through the years?

18) Research and report on paintings that have families in them. What does the painting tell us about the families and how they lived?

19) Research famous women artists. What difficulties did they encounter as women? Write a report about why art is important. Take a painting and tell how it changed peoples' lives.

20) Research the history of fashion. How does the design of clothing reflect the people and periods in which they were worn? What was life like when women wore long dresses? Consider what the Muslim women wear (bourkas). What does this tell you about the women of Muslim faith and how they live each day?

21) Research different kinds of government and tell why government affects the art of the country.

22) Research and report on a famous poet. Select some of the poet's poetry. What does it tell you about the poet and the way he lived?

23) Research and report on a country's fairytales and myths. What do they tell you about the way people thought and lived?

24) Research impressionist painters other than Monet and compare their work to an artist of a later period. What makes their art different? Which one do you prefer? How can you tell them apart?

25) Research Miró or Klee and tell what you like and/or dislike about their art.

26) Rodan created a great sculpture. Research his life and tell why you like or dislike his artwork.

27) Research the Guggenheim Museum in Spain. Tell whether you like or dislike this type of architecture. Compare it to the great cathedrals of medieval times. Which do you like better? Explain your reasons.

28) Research the art forms of today (Op art, Pop art, Abstract art, Surrealism). Compare them to classic or romantic art forms. Give your opinion of both and tell what you like or dislike about them.

29) Research Escher and explain what influenced his art and explain what makes it so unusual. Tell whether you like or dislike his artwork.

30) Research optical illusions and tell how they are used in artwork today. Give examples.

31) Research the designs of different cars and how they have changed over the years. How do you think they will change in the future? Show your research to support your ideas.

CREATIVE PROJECTS

1) Paint three paintings, each representing a different period of art. Tell the difference.

2) Create a sculpture and tell what time period it represents.

3) Design coins for our world today and for another period of your choice.

4) Make a book of one or more artists, telling about the painting and about the artist who painted it.

5) Some art is very exacting. Using a ruler and pencil, draw a picture that shows perspective.

6) Make up a story about Van Gogh's "Starry Night" or "Potato Eaters." What do you think Van Gogh wanted you to see when he painted this?

7) Make a mobile and bring it to class to share.

8) If you had $100,000,000, what art would you buy? Write about your choices.

9) Look for beautiful treasured items and take pictures of them. Make a scrapbook.

10) Create three musical instruments. Play them. What are their names?

11) Select five paintings and write a poem for each one.

12) Many artists painted self-portraits. Pick two that you like, and tell us what they say about the artists. Then draw a self-portrait and ask the class to tell what your picture says about you.

13) Surrealism is about dreams and symbolism. Create a picture that tells a dream world of yours. Include in it at least four symbols.

14) Watch how the light changes color. Choose a subject and color it in the early morning, mid-afternoon, and early evening.

15) Make a scrapbook of photographs that you have taken. Write a small paragraph or poem about each photograph and tell why you chose each photograph for your scrapbook. Take pictures of common objects in new and different ways.

16) Create a collage of different styles of art.

17) Make a relief from clay or similar material.

18) Make a model of a future car and tell what new changes have been added.

19) Create a cartoon character and make seven comic strips of at least four pictures about him or her.

20) Write a story about foreign intrigue and art (i.e. How the Mona Lisa was stolen and recovered.) This could also involve Power Point presentations on the computer.

21) Design six costumes for a king or queen that lived in 17th, 18th, 19th or 20th century and tell where they would wear them.

22) Write and illustrate a book on a famous American artist's life.

23) Make a book containing a minimum of 12 art activities. Explain in detail how to do them.

24) Create your own board game about art and/or artists

25) Compose a piece of music. Tape or play it for the class.

26) Create a catalog of at least twenty gifts from a famous art museum.

27) Pretend you are a person in a painting. Write a story about how it feels and what was going on after the painting was completed.

28) Great artists have lived throughout the world. Find out where at least ten famous European artists lived, and make a map showing where each was born.

29) Dress up like a character in a famous painting, and tell us about the painting and the artist.

30) Create an art calendar with a picture for each month. Mark the birthdays of at least fifteen famous artists.

31) Create a three-dimensional dream house.

32) Create a robot for the future using buttons, plastic beads, foil, etc.

33) Use photographs to tell a story about a real-life event.

34) Frank Lloyd Wright was a famous architect who modeled his buildings after forms in nature. Design a school that represents a form in nature. What new things would there be in it that we do not have today?

35) Make your own paper. Give us the steps you followed to make it and draw something on it.

36) Go to a nearby museum and think about what it would be like to have the people in the paintings come alive. Tell us about a night in your museum by writing a story with pictures.

37) Research portraits. Select two that you like best and tell what the paintings communicate about the person in the picture. Are they happy, sad? Why? What does the color and background do to tell more about the person in the painting?

38) Look through an art book and find a painting that brings out your inner feelings. Does it make you happy, sad, mad? Who is

the artist and how did he make you feel the way you did? Why do you think the artist painted that painting?

39) Look through an art book for paintings of light. How does the artist paint the light? Is there a sun in the painting? Are there shadows in the painting? Write about this topic.

Making dreams come true in paint

Making self-portrait sculptures from plaster

These are only suggestions to an unlimited amount of choices. The purpose of these reports is not simply to gather words and write them down. It is to read, think, interpret, understand, and apply information in a practical way. It is important for each report to show that the student has used their own reasoning to write the paper, which will help them form values and answers for their own lives. An "A" will only be given to those students who follow the directions above.

CHAPTER 11

WORLD GEOGRAPHY

MAIN OBJECTIVE

This is a great unit to expose students to the world and the people in it. We look at the problems facing our future and work to find answers. We learn about diverse cultures on each of the seven continents, and how they were formed. We also learn about the layers of earth, including what causes mountains and earthquakes.

At the beginning of the year, each student received a poster board with longitude and latitude lines representing every 15 degrees. As we studied each continent, we cut out its shape and placed it on its proper location on the poster board, which became a world map. Near the end of the year we added oceans, islands, and other details we had studied. To color oceans, I got blue tissue paper and plastic bags. The students put their hands in the bags so that the dye couldn't color their hands. They dampened the tissue in water and blotted the board to color it blue. The lines of longitude and latitude were drawn with permanent black markers that did not affect the tissue. This made the map look realistic and was quick to do. Make sure each student has his/her name written on the back of their map. Otherwise, they will be hard to tell apart. Do not let students glue their continents on the map until you have checked to make sure they are placed correctly.

This unit lends itself well to guest speakers. If you know of people, including parents, from another country, invite them to talk to the class. We had a multicultural organization that loved sending speakers. They brought samples and pictures. We had high tea services from England and Japan. We also found a tea house and visited it on a field trip—- a very special day!

This unit is great for setting up debates and trials. Students enjoyed both. The political situation in Ireland offered a great debate topic. So was immigration. Trials are also fun. Appoint a judge, jury, lawyers for opening and closing arguments, and witnesses. Students love role playing. A good trial could be a person caught on a country's land and accused of spying, or a painting by Picasso found in someone's house, resulting in that person being accused of stealing, while the person said it was a gift. Another debate topic could be the pollution of a stream blamed on a factory that denied responsibility. Another good topic for debate is whether or not to preserve rainforests.

A great unit to do on rainforests is to get a big refrigerator box and divide it into four compartments representing the levels of a rainforest. I colored the background and added a three-dimensional tree. Have the class research, choose and create an animal that lives in one of the four levels by using colored paper, tissue, glitter, sequins, and puff balls. Each child's animal is then placed in one of the four levels of the rainforest, along with a description of the animal attached to it. It was a beautiful addition for our study of South America, Africa, and Asia. Students learned to appreciate all the life in the rainforest and to understand how important it is to preserve each.

When studying Australia, collect long cardboard rolls from a drapery store that sells material. This must be collected early in the year. It takes time to collect enough for the whole class. Discuss Aborigines of Australia and make didgeridoos and rain sticks. Decorate them as you study the artwork of these people. Ask someone who can play a didgeridoo or get a recording of this, so the class can try to play them.

The U.N. has activities for children. We organized a meeting with another school and presented reports asking for funds and for clean water, etc. If you look this up, you'll find it is a great thing to do.

Playing their didgeridoos

MULTICULTURAL DAY

This is a school-wide activity. Invite people from different countries to visit classrooms during the day, listing them by time on a sign-up sheet. Talk to international restaurants in the area. Ask them to visit the school on that day. After students eat lunch, they are invited to go outside where restaurants are set up. Students can circulate around to each one and sample food. We had Mexican, Italian, Asian, Indian, and German food. The students loved this. But it was not easy to organize. If you have a multicultural club in your school, it would be easier to partner with them for this project.

SUCCESSFUL ACTIVITIES

1) Stage a debate and a court drama.

2) Create a rainforest.

3) Participate in a U.N. activity.

4) Create a volcano erupting.

5) Make didgeridoos and rain sticks.

6) Quiz Bowl.

7) Make different sized circles and color them to represent the street, city, state, country, continent, earth, universe.

EXTRA MATERIALS

1) Poster boards for each student

2) Tissue paper that bleeds its color

3) Plastic bags

4) Clay

5) Baking powder (for volcanoes)

6) Vinegar (for volcanoes)

7) A refrigerator box

8) Colored papers

9) Puffballs

10) Feathers

11) Glue

12) Scissors

13) Sequins

14) Permanent markers

15) 3-foot cardboard tubes or plastic from Home Depot

16) Book from a library about various topics and continents

FIELD TRIPS

1) Supermarket to discover food from all over the world

2) Attend the Nutcracker Ballet

3) Ethnic restaurants

4) Folk festivals

GUEST SPEAKERS

1) Someone from a country other than the United States

2) A U.N. representative

3) A didgeridoo player

QUIZ BOWL

The following are sample questions you may use.

1) Where is the equator?

2) Where on earth does the day begin first?

3) Name the seven continents.

4) What continent is also a country?

5) Name the oceans.

6) Who are the Aborigines?

7) What is a didgeridoo?

8) What is the United Nations?

9) What is the difference between communism and democracy?

10) Where would you find the Amazon River?

11) Where is the Nile River?

12) Where are the Himalayan Mountains?

13) Where are the Rocky Mountains?

14) Where are the Azores?

15) How many countries are there in the world today?

16) Name a country next to France.

17) What is the Russian Federation?

18) What is a burka?

19) What is the world's second largest democracy?

20) What four countries are called the Scandinavian countries?

21) Name one problem that Africa faces.

22) Which is the coldest pole on earth?

23) Name the four parts of the rainforest.(emergent, canopy, understory, floor)

TREASURE HUNT

Sean tied down the last flap on his backpack and checked to make sure he had his compass in his right pocket. He had already said goodbye to his family. It was finally time to leave on a worldwide journey. He was excited but a little scared until I told him you would be helping him.

1) Sean will be visiting all the continents. Name them.

2) There is a list of things Sean will need. Unscramble them. coat; shoes; raincoat; sleeping bag.

3) Where does every day on earth begin?

4) What would you find in King Tut's tomb?

5) What continent is owned by numerous different countries together?

6) What is latitude?

7) What is longitude?

8) What line divides the world in half going east and west?

9) Who makes didgeridoos?

10) Where would Sean find the longest river in the world?

11) Make up a ten-line song about a rainforest to the tune of "You Are My Sunshine." Everyone on your team should sing this together so Sean can hear it.

12) What would you want to say to the Queen of England?

13) What would you want Sean to see once you have gotten to North America?

14) Choose the favorite thing that you would like and draw a picture of it.

15) Sean is definitely going to climb the tallest mountain in the world. Tell what mountain it is and write down two things he would see during his journey.

16) To get from North America to Europe, which ocean must Sean cross?

17) What wall can be seen from space and where would you find it?

18) What continent is also a country name?

19) Name three animals you would find there and tell something about each one.

20) Where would you find whales in the summer?

21) Sean is on his way home. He took pictures of his favorite continent. Show us four of those pictures.

22) Something blew on our lawn from another continent. Find this item. Tell where it came from and what on Earth it is.

23) Put all your things together and clean up. Come to me for your final check.

RESEARCH PAPER TOPICS

Listed below are several topics you may use for your research report. REMINDER: A third of your paper should be ideas that support the issue; and a third should state your opinion about the issue. If you would like to report on a topic not listed below, please see me before you begin.

1) Research the history of the Aborigines in Australia. Do you think the modern world can help the Aborigines maintain their way of life?

2) Research the culture of an immigrant worker in America and/ or around the world. What are the good points and what are the problems of having immigrants in a country? What do you think should be done about this issue?

3) Research the Olympics. Do you think they are a good or bad influence for the world?

4) There are many children in the world with neither a mother nor father to care for them. Should we try to help them or just let them roam the streets?

5) Rainforests are being cut down. Is this a good thing or a bad thing?

6) Nuclear power plants help us with our energy, but some people think they are dangerous. List the good and bad points of this issue and give your opinion.

7) World hunger is a huge problem. Is food with high sugar content good or bad in helping solve this problem?

8) Palestine. Should there be an independent state for the Palestinians or not?

9) Recycling. Is it a good thing or just a waste of time?

10) Global warming. Is it real or not? If it is real what can we do about it?

11) Shark tail soup. Good or bad?

12) What happens when large stores like Wal-Mart move into a small town? Is it a good thing or bad?

13) Children around the world are forced to work long hours in factories. List the good points and bad points of this issue. What is your opinion?

14) Is it important to help animals that provide food for us to have a happy life? How are chickens kept that supply eggs for the stores? Should cows be fed corn?

15) Should pesticides be used in food growing?

CREATIVE REPORT TOPICS

1) Design a peace poster to be used for world peace, and write at least four steps that we could do for world peace. Give a talk explaining your ideas.

2) Make three posters for saving endangered species or helping animals that have been treated unkindly. Write a talk to give to your class about this subject.

3) Design a place for chickens to live where they can be happy and lay eggs for stores. Make a diorama of your idea.

4) Make a space ship and write a story about the future in space. Tell at least five ways that it would affect life on earth.

5) Make a diorama of a rainforest with four layers including animals that live in each layer.

6) Write a story about an immigrant coming to America.

7) Make a diagram of a nuclear power plant.

8) Make a cookbook for organic foods. Make at least one recipe and bring it to share with the class.

9) Make recycling posters to put up around the school. Make a cartoon explaining the history and need for recycling. Your cartoon should have a superhero that you make up.

10) Make a list of things we can do to prevent global warming. Create a pop-up book illustrating your ideas. Ask for examples for your pop-up book.

11) Make a puppet play of a child who had to work in a factory and how they helped children like them find a better life.

12) Make some drawings that could come from the Aborigines in Australia. Explain your drawings to the class and tell us about how the drawings teach us about the Aborigines and how they live.

13) Create a story about someone taking a trip around the world. The story must be illustrated and be at least 100 words in length.

14) Write about a new country that you created. In your story you could include the following: a flag, currency, colors, mascot, flower, bird, and logo. What would their national sport and pastime be? Where would your country be located and who would live there?

15) Write and perform a play about a country or place you would like to visit.

16) Write a story about an adventure in a country of your dreams.

17) Make a Power Point presentation about our world.

18) Create a comic book about someone living on another continent.

19) Create a gift that you would send to a person in another country. Write a story about what happened to it.

20) Create a musical instrument and make up a story about its interesting past and future.

21) Create a super hero that travels across the earth helping during natural disasters. What can this super hero do and what does he or she look like? Take us on an adventure where his or her powers stop a tragedy.

22) Rewrite the story "Goodnight Moon" and rename it "Goodnight Earth." Illustrate it.

23) Oops! There is a book missing in the Star Wars Trilogy. It was found buried in the snow on top of Mount Everest. It was entitled "Star Wars – Where the Earth Meets the Sky." Write and illustrate this lost book.

24) Find three pieces of art from different places around the world and make up a story about each picture.

25) Make at least three different crafts from three different countries around the world. Be ready to explain what these crafts tell you about the people and the way they live.

CHAPTER 12

LIVING THINGS LARGE AND SMALL

MAIN OBJECTIVE:

A unit dedicated to all living things, this unit focuses on building an awareness of and appreciation for our world, its beauty, and balance. Students will grow in the understanding of the role they can play in maintaining their earth and all its living things.

Activities include microscopic animals (using a microscope and pond water), bees, ants, spiders, butterflies, cockroaches, termites, deer, bears, sharks, endangered species, whales, dolphins, the food chain, and saving our oceans.

SUCCESSFUL ACTIVITIES

1) Have an ant farm in class to observe.

2) Construct an insect hotel a place to attract insects, using food, seeds, etc. Have a contest to see whose hotel would have the most insects at the end of one week.

3) Learn parts of a microscopic and how to use one. Observe amoebas and other microscopic animals. Draw pictures of them.

4) Have an aquarium in the classroom.

5) Make a 3-D stuffed whale with bulletin board paper and newspaper.

6) Have a pet show.

7) Order caterpillars and observe how they turn into butterflies.

8) Watch a mealworm go through metamorphosis and observe its movement. Give everyone a mealworm to take home. Put the mealworms in small containers with corn meal.

EXTRA MATERIALS

1) Materials to make bug houses

2) Microscopes

3) Corn meal container for mealworm

4) Pond water

5) Incubator (full section on chickens will follow)

GUEST SPEAKER

1) Pest control person

2) Beekeeper

3) Humane Society or Sierra Club representative

4) Embryology expert

FIELD TRIPS

1) Any science museum that features animals

2) Marine Science facility such as Sea World

3) Local farm open to children.

4) Find a science center that will dissect sharks.

TREASURE HUNT

The world depends on animals large and small to survive. We are experiencing some extreme weather problems, and many species are becoming extinct. This is of great concern to us all. Your team has joined up with an organization desperately trying to save animal life on earth. You have been given a list of things to do to help our world.

1) Name an animal that is on the endangered list. What is one thing we can do to save it?

2) Ants are an incredible insect. Name five different jobs that need to be done in an ant colony so it can survive. Draw an ant doing a job.

3) You are going hunting to find certain animals. You will need to take some things along, but they get all mixed up. (Note: Scramble the following words for the class to unscramble. Camera, shovel, mosquito net, binoculars, bug book.)

4) Which animal travels 5000 miles every year to eat what?

5) Which animal hibernates and has babies in the cold winter?

6) Which insect has a queen as big as a hot dog?

7) What happens to a bee if it stings you?

8) Why would a poacher kill an elephant? What can be done to prevent this?

9) Your team needs to pick an animal species to save. Make a poster to tell people what they can do to join you to save this animal.

10) What is metamorphosis? Tell one animal that goes through metamorphosis. Draw it in four stages.

11) What is partial metamorphosis? Which animal goes through this?

12) What is the difference between a moth and a butterfly? Tell three things about each one.

13) Write an eight-line poem that rhymes, to the tune of "Twinkle, Twinkle Little Star." Your whole group must sing the song together.

14) Write a thank you note to our school custodian, thanking him for keeping our campus free of harmful spiders, etc.

15) Pick up at least ten pieces of litter around the school to help it stay clean and bug free.

16) Draw a fish that is keeping our oceans clean. How many of these fish are killed every year to make ________________? (Note: shark tail soup)

17) What is the largest creature on earth? What does it eat?

18) Does your team think it's okay that Sea World and the circus use animals to entertain people? If yes, say why. If not, give reasons.

19) What do spiders do for us?

20) There is a world that exists in our oceans that we know little about. There are fish that produce their own light called ____________________. (bioluminescence)

QUIZ BOWL QUESTIONS YOU MAY USE

1) What is a microscope?

2) What is an amoeba?

3) How does a single celled animal reproduce?

4) How many legs does an insect have?

5) How many body parts does an insect have?

6) What does a queen ant do all day?

7) How big is a queen termite?

8) Does the termite eat wood?

9) What is metamorphosis?

10) Name the four stages of metamorphosis.

11) What is the difference between a moth and a butterfly?

12) What does a monarch butterfly eat?

13) What is royal jelly?

14) How do bees keep cool in the summer sun?

15) Name an animal that starts out in the water and later flies with wings.

16) What is an owl pellet?

17) A frog starts out swimming in a pond as a ______________(tadpole)

18) What insect throws up everywhere?

19) How many days does it take a chicken to hatch?

20) Only __________ (female) mosquitoes bite humans.

21) Elephants are killed for their ______________(tusks).

22) What does habitat mean?

23) Name an endangered species.

24) What animals have become extinct?

25) If humans would eat insects, people would never go __________ (hungry).

26) Name a good thing about sharks.

27) What is a baleen whale?

28) What is the largest living thing on earth today?

29) True or false: Under the Gulf of Mexico, there is a lake whose density is so strong that it exists apart from the water surrounding it.

30) What does "bio" mean?

31) Does life exist in the ocean without sunlight?

32) There is fire under the ocean. It comes from __________ (underwater volcanoes).

33) What is the deepest part of the earth? Where would you find it? Does anything live there?

34) What is bioluminescence?

RESEARCH PAPER TOPICS

1) Pick an insect that you would like to know more about (do not pick one that we are studying in class). What did you learn about this insect that you didn't know before? In your opinion is this a good or bad insect and tell why.

2) Insects and animals all behave in unexplainable, seemingly intelligent ways. What or why do you think living things act the way they do without ever going to school or watching TV? Tell some examples of insect behaviors.

3) Do you think that animals are influenced by their great, great, great, great ancestors? There are no history books for them to read. Research the personalities of different dogs and give your opinion about why they behave in different ways.

4) Animal life that we cannot see without a microscope is awesome. Research this kind of life and tell how you think it survives. Do you think that animals that are so small are important? Why or why not? How or what can we do to help them to survive when we cannot see them?

5) Research animals that are on the endangered species list. Give your opinion on how we can save these animals and why you think it is important to do so.

6) Research various ecosystems and tell about the animals that live in them. Many of these ecosystems are being destroyed to make way for industry and factories. Do you feel this is a good or bad thing? Give your opinion as to how important these ecosystems are and what, if anything, can be done to save them.

7) Research the Everglades and the conflict between it and the sugar cane industry. State your opinion as to which side you support.

8) Research desalination and decide whether you think it is good or bad and tell why.

9) Research an animal that has taken on different forms to adapt to its changing environment and forecast which animals will change in the future and tell how.

10) Pick an insect you think is most important to our world and tell why you chose this insect. Make your argument convincing. Do you think insects act out of intelligence or instinct? Give examples to support your opinion.

11) If people would eat insects there would be enough food to feed the world. How would you convince the world's population to accept this idea? Do you think this is a good or bad idea?

12) Many insects can be harmful. Research some of these creatures and tell what things to be careful about. Tell where to find these insects and how to identify them. Do you think we should exterminate these insects? What would happen if we did?

13) Research global warming and tell how it could affect us and our future. Tell what we can do about it.

14) Many animals are extinct or are becoming extinct. Tell the consequences of an animal that has become extinct or is becoming extinct. How does it affect you? How does it affect our future?

CREATIVE PROJECTS

Here is a list of possible creative projects:

1) Pick an animal on the endangered species list and take it to the mall. Dress your animal in the latest fashions. Tell how each outfit that you pick will help your chosen animal protect themselves from the dangers they face. Keep in mind camouflage. (Pick at least five outfits.)

2) Invent and create something that will help the world help its animals. Tell why your invention will make a difference.

3) Create an advertising campaign informing your school about the importance of all living things. Write announcements. Make a poster. Write something for the newsletter or local newspaper.

4) Make up your own newsletter about insects, spiders, and bugs. Include a word search, puzzle, and an interview with people about bugs. Name a "Superstar Bug."

5) Take pictures of bugs in your neighborhood. Tell why you think they live where they do and explain to the class some of their habits you have observed.

6) Make a list of over twenty-five bugs. Tell what each does that is good and what each does that is not so good.

7) Design an ideal habitat for an animal or insect. You need to make a 3-D model. Please do not use Legos or store-bought models.

8) Create three special kinds of music for three or more different animals. Tell why you made the music sound the way it does and why you think the creature you made it for would like it.

9) Make up a contest for the greatest insect idol. Who is in the contest and who will win? Draw or write about this story. You must have at least seven contestants.

10) You are a producer who has been chosen to make up a movie for the upcoming "Survivor Show." Pretend that you're a bug. What bugs will you choose for your show? What challenges will you give them? Where will it take place and who will win the million dollars? What will the winner do with the money?

11) Make up a TV news special for bugs. All the characters must be bugs including two anchors, a sports writer, a weather forecaster, and national reporter. Who are the advertisers? What is the lead story for the day? You may draw, write, or record it on a VHS tape.

12) Make up a story about how a bug got into a video game and how he finally escaped. Use illustrations to support your theme.

13) Pretend you have been shrunk to the size of a grasshopper. Tell what your world would be like and write a story about your adventures.

14) Think of a favorite fairytale. Change the story and replace the main characters with an insect. Example: The Three Little Caterpillars, Goldilocks and the Three Ants. Write and illustrate your story.

15) Make a model that is an example of global warming. Show how it has made a difference to an animal.

16) Create a mystery with fish living in the deepest part of the ocean as the main characters. Illustrate your story

CHAPTER 13

COMMUNICATION AND INVENTIONS

MAIN OBJECTIVE

Greatness comes from our inner passion and our ability to express qualities that we share with each other. Doors open to new pathways and understanding with this unit. Studying qualities that others express will help students appreciate and value the sacrifices of others and to honor their accomplishments. Researching inventors and great leaders will stress the character traits that made them successful. Students will also discover that it is not the accumulation of material things that gives us true success and happiness. It is the desire to help make a difference in the world. Students learn that their choices in life will mold their future and help develop greatness in themselves. They learn about the needs of humanity. Through this study, students develop a sensitivity to the problems surrounding the future of our planet and learn to use their creative skills to think into the future for ways to solve issues we will face. They will learn to appreciate their own unique qualities and see them as gifts that will enrich their own personal lives and the lives of all mankind. This unit explores simple inventions by taking them apart to see what makes them work. Students create their own inventions and make sculptures from other inventions they have taken apart.

ACTIVITIES

1) Study the qualities of Abraham Lincoln.

2) Study Helen Keller. Watch the movie "Miracle Worker." What made Helen Keller great?

3) Learn some Braille.

4) Learn some sign language.

5) Bring in broken appliances and tools to take them apart.

6) Create sculptures using pieces from appliances we took apart.

7) Make an invention and enter it in an invention fair at school and elsewhere.

8) Have a famous person night. Everyone dresses up as a famous person and comes prepared to answer questions about the character as parents and friends visit and have refreshments.

9) Make puppets and write a play about leadership and learning life lessons. Present your play to other classes.

10) Tape plays so the class can see its own plays.

11) Make ice cream in plastic bags.

12) Bring in gadgets and have the class guess what they are used for.

13) Study inventions that were originally mistakes, such as chocolate chip cookies, milk bottles, Lifesavers, and Ivory Soap.

14) Invent something to drop from a high spot with a raw egg and see who invented something that kept the egg from breaking. (no bubble wrap.)

15) Discuss the development of civilization. What did inventions have to do with how our lives changed

16) Inventions in the future: How will our world change? What inventions will there be?

17) Debate: What is the world's greatest invention?

18) Have a fashion show with students wearing homemade clothes from recycled material.

GUEST SPEAKERS

1) Invite a deaf and/or blind person to talk to the class, and discuss inventions that have helped them, along with what things they could have that would help them more.

2) Find an inventor to talk to the class.

INVENTING AN ICE CREAM DISH

1) Ask parents to donate some things a couple of weeks before this activity. You may need to get some items that are missing – especially the milk.

2) Gallon plastic bags that can be sealed tightly.

3) Storage plastic bags (slightly smaller than 1 gallon). These bags need to be tightly sealed. Do not get inexpensive plastic bags. You need good, thick plastic bags that will not break.

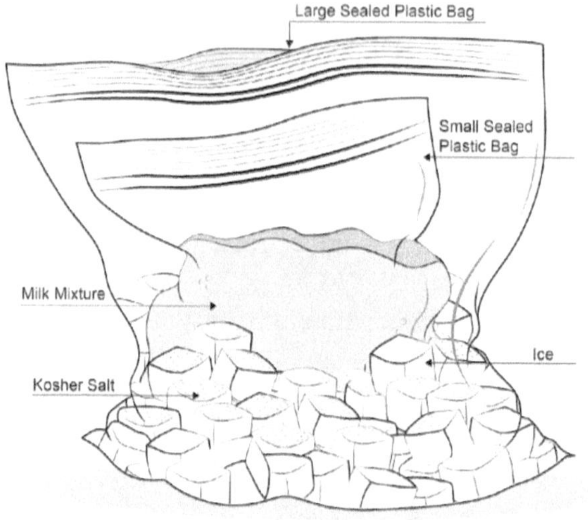

4) A gallon of milk for every class.

5) Sugar

6) Vanilla

7) Salt

8) Ice

9) Food coloring

10) Bowls

11) Whipped cream

12) Cherries

13) Spoons

14) Variety of toppings

15) Gloves

MEASURING

Put 1-1/2 cup milk in each storage bag. Add two tsp sugar and one tsp vanilla. You can also add food coloring. Seal bag. Put ice in every gallon bag. Add salt to the ice. Add the milk bag, sealed, into the gallon bag and seal. Now, shake and shake and shake until the milk turns into ice cream. Gloves help keep hands warm. Empty ice cream into a bowl and top with whatever you have. Limit the students to three items. Have the students name their ice cream creation and enjoy. The students love this noisy, fun activity. They can draw it with its name under their picture. (For other recipes, google "ice cream in a bag.")

Watch that the bags are completely sealed. Getting ice water into the milk mixture will ruin everything. Be ready to help students re-do this if necessary.

Discuss why the salt is important. Ask if anyone wants to make the ice cream without using salt in it. Let them try if they want to. Explain that when you add salt to the ice, you melt the ice. But before it melts, it gets colder, and this extreme cold is what enables the milk to turn into ice cream. It causes a chemical reaction. Discuss the salt trucks that go out in the snow to put salt on the roads to help the snow melt for drivers.

RESEARCH REPORT FOR INVENTIONS

1) Research schools for blind and/or deaf children. How are they different from regular schools? What can they do to earn a living when they are out of school? How do you think we can help them?

2) Think about your favorite invention. Who invented it, and what motivated him/her to create it? Research the problems that had to be overcome to make the invention successful. How do you think it will change in the future?

3) Research a famous person and tell why s/he became famous. What qualities did this person have that you admire? How will these qualities help you in the future?

4) Research some famous black inventors and tell about their work. What problems did they have? What do you think it would be like to be a black inventor today?

5) Research the history of language. How many different languages are there? Why do you think there are so many?

6) Research communication. Write about how people have learned to communicate and to understand each other when they are so different. What do you think is the best way to communicate? Why? How has it helped?

7) Many inventions that have been successful started as mistakes. Research an invention that started out as a mistake and tell what happened that made it succeed. Tell of a mistake you have made and how it ended up being a good thing after all.

8) Research people who are working on inventions. What are the problems they face? Do you think their ideas will succeed? If not, why?

9) Research the relationship between Henry Ford and Thomas Edison. What did these two men have in common that made them great? Which one do you like best? Why?

10) Thomas Edison had many inventions we do not even know about. Research some of these inventions and tell which ones you like best.

11) Leonardo da Vinci invented some things used in wars. What were they? What do you think about him as an inventor?

12) Research the food industry and tell how food packaging and distribution have changed. Do you think this is good or not so good?

CREATIVE PROJECTS FOR INVENTIONS

1) Make a book for a blind child.

2) Invent a helpful invention for a child who cannot hear.

3) Write a story about how an invention came to life and what happened to it.

4) Make a book of qualities that makes someone successful.

5) Make a timeline of the most important inventions. Tell why you picked the ones that you did.

6) Make up a puppet play of a famous person and present it to the class.

7) Make a book of poems that you like that tell about famous people, or about qualities that you admire.

8) Choose a problem in the world that you would like to solve. Invent something that would help solve the problem and tell how it would work.

9) We have a big, diverse world with many different languages. Create a universal alphabet. Make a book illustrating each letter.

TREASURE HUNT

You have been hired to build a museum for the world's most uncelebrated inventions. Your mission is to collect the inventions that will inspire the world and hopefully help make it a better place.

1) Help people like Helen Keller learn Braille. Write "I love you" in Braille.

2) An invention has been found in a corner of a little town. It is square and holds something strange inside. Create this odd thing and tell what you think it is and how it can be used.

3) Abraham Lincoln was an honest, hardworking man who gave up his own feelings about war to save our country. Find something that shows Lincoln's greatness to put in your museum. It should inspire us to follow his example.

4) In the great outdoors, there are wonderful possibilities for our future progress. Find something outside and tell what it could do to help others.

5) Walt Disney was inspired by a little mouse. It was the beginning of a bright, wonderful career. Select an animal that inspires you. Name it and tell how it could give you a successful career.

6) Write a thank you note to a great person on campus. Give the person the note and have him/her sign a paper saying s/he got the note. You cannot go inside a classroom where a teacher is teaching. A custodian, cafeteria worker, counselor, office person, or someone in the media center would be best.

7) No one knows it, but what seems to be litter has the potential for an incredible invention. Pick up a piece of litter and transform it into an amazing invention.

8) Write a song at least eight lines long to the tune of "You are My Sunshine." The poem needs to rhyme and be about an invention everyone needs. Sing it together.

9) An inventor needs many things. Help unscramble these things so you know what they are: screwdriver, paper, glue, pencil, a dream, work room.

10) Thomas Edison and Henry Ford lived next door to each other in Fort Myers. If you were a little mouse hiding near where the two famous men would sit to watch the sun go down at night, what would you hear them talking about? Write a paragraph of a conversation that you imagine existed between these two men.

11) Thomas Edison collected plants from all over the world for his experiments. Pick something outside or inside and tell what good you think it might do.

12) Many fruits have been put together with other fruits to make new fruits. A peach and a plum put together is a nectarine. What two things would you put together? By doing so, what would you get? Name your new fruit. Draw it.

13) Water is a necessity. Without it, we cannot live. Some people do not have clean water to drink. You are out to help the world get water that is clean to drink. Write about your plan and tell how you will get clean water. 14)You need to gather all your items and glue them in your museum. Name your museum. Bring it up to be checked and to get your final puzzle piece.

QUIZ BOWL

Here are some Quiz Bowl questions for a unit on Inventors and Communication:

1) Name a quality of greatness.

2) What made Abraham Lincoln great?

3) What was the Civil War about?

4) How many times did Thomas Edison try to invent the electric light bulb?

5) Helen Keller had two main disabilities. What were they?

6) What happened to Helen Keller that made her understand the world around her?

7) What made Helen Keller great?

8) Who was Helen Keller's teacher?

9) Name a famous inventor other than Thomas Edison. Tell what he invented.

10) Our world has changed greatly because of many inventions. Name something that almost disappeared after the invention of plumbing, electricity and light bulbs, or cars.

11) What became popular after Toll House cookies became popular?

12) Name an invention that turned out to be a big hit but was a mistake to begin with.

13) What two important inventions were thought to make the modern world what it is today?

14) What is your favorite invention? Why?

15) Walt Disney invented a character that put Disney on the map. Who was the character?

16) What is Braille?

17) If you could make an invention for the future, what would it be?

TREASURE HUNT — FOR YOUNGER GRADES

It was a strange morning. The sky was shining with a mysterious mist in the air. The birds were not to be heard. Silence was everywhere. You decided to go outside to see what was going on. The newspaper in your driveway has huge, bold headlines – "STUDENTS LOST IN TIME MACHINE. WE DON'T KNOW WHERE THEY ARE OR HOW TO GET THEM BACK." "We have received a message, which includes directions that will insure the children's safe return and uncovering a **treasure.**

CLUES

1) The wheel is one of the world's most important inventions. Draw three things that were invented because of the wheel.

2) Henry Ford invented something that changed the world. What did he invent?

3) Some great inventions have given our world joy and fun. Walt Disney created some characters. Unscramble the following characters: Donald Duck; Mickey Mouse; Miss Piggy

ADDLON–KUDC/CMIEYK–EUMOS/SMSI-GPGYI

4) Thomas Edison and Alexander Graham Bell helped shape the world we live in. Name something each of them invented.

5) A super hero is hungry. He is willing to use his energy and might to help bring the children home. Set a dinner table for him by drawing the following items in your book: a dinner plate, salad plate, drinking glass, napkin, teaspoon, soup spoon, fork, salad fork, and knife.

6) Gratitude is an important quality. Write two identical thank you notes to give to a staff member at school. Do not interrupt

a classroom. The note must include at least one quality that the person expresses. Have them sign one of them and return it to the person in charge.

7) In order to find the children, we are going to need a sense of time. This way we will be able to track them down. Make a list of the following events or things in the order in which they happened: electric light, beginning of language, U.S.A., stone tools, TV.

8) Create two special effects and tell how they will help the children.

9) Many inventions were created to help others. Make an invention using something from litter around the school that will help make the world a better place to live. Do not use any living plant or object. Tell how it will help.

10) Entertainment plays an important part in our everyday life. In order to bring the children back safely you need to sing them a song. Make up a song that is four lines long to the tune of "Twinkle Twinkle Little Star" and sing it as a group.

11) Music is a universal language. Create a musical instrument from nature and tell what qualities it expresses when you play it.

12) Everyone in your group needs to draw a picture of your favorite invention.

13) Clean up your work areas, assemble your book, and turn it in for your last puzzle piece.

CHAPTER 14

WRITING

It was brutally unpopular. Most of my gifted students disliked writing more than anything else I asked them to do. It all started when teachers were required to instruct their students in a way that made writing structured. Children were deprived of their innovative creative spirit and writing became pure drudgery. Something had to be done to loosen up the wonderful imaginative minds of my students, so they could discover the joys of words and thoughts they had to share. I loved and believed in their potential and didn't want to abandon their talents, nor did I want to deprive them of the benefits that came with inspired writing. I dedicated the last half hour of each day to journal writing. This time was for students to write about their day or anything they wanted to share.

The paper they wrote on was the back side of a logic puzzle completed earlier in the day. The puzzle was a challenge and required a lot of mental concentration. If they figured it out successfully, they would get a sticker, which was the indicator of their accomplishment and enabled them to get a piece of candy from a jar on my desk. Disappointed with the quality of the journal writing, I searched for a way to encourage my students to demonstrate the level of excellence I expected. The solution to the problem was obvious. The journal had to be written neatly, and it had to have the correct number of words. If it was not up to the standard, they did not get a sticker and thus were deprived of the coveted piece of candy. This put an end to the half-written, scrabbled journals. I no longer read sentences that were cut off in the middle because the required number of words had been reached. I no longer saw papers with words magnified to unnatural heights to fill the page with as few words as possible. It also put an end to "I had a very, very, very, very, very nice day." The journals became more than a dumb thing they had to do at the end of each day, they became a priority. I was on a mission much larger than forcing my students to write a real journal. They knew the expectations and had forced themselves to conform so they could get a piece of candy. I had witnessed the contempt and then the conformity to the writing skills they had been forced to work with. I didn't want to reinforce this teaching and continue their dislike of writing. That was the last thing I wanted to do.

I remembered when I first began to teach and my students loved to write. I cherished the books we printed with student poems, thoughts, and illustrations. We had sold them for an economic project and I had won a national award for the effort. What had happened to change things? I didn't want to conform to a system that was draining my students of their love for writing. Their individuality didn't need to follow a prescribed format. Their spirit was being buried under mounds of rules and tests and was void of originality. Writing had become an array of words marching in conformity —mindless, lifeless, and totally boring. To raise my gifted, talented students' creative abilities from extinction, I had to find a way to bring excitement back into their pencils. I wanted to open their inner uniqueness and offer them the opportunity to express and discover a whole new world within themselves. Writing about their day just wasn't doing the trick.

I gathered each of my classes together and told them about my feelings. I wanted to change their attitudes toward writing. Comparing words to colors on an artist's canvas, I explained that writing was another way of creating scenes. It was painting pictures with words. We also discussed the easy flow of words that came to them as they talked to a friend. If they could begin to think of writing as a conversation, the words would unfold naturally like the petals of a flower realizing its full potential and beauty. It was easy and fun. I told them to give writing a whole new chance promising that they might even start to enjoy it. I picked new, unusual topics and asked them to write about things that would inspire their imaginations and spark their desire to share their souls. The structured format was removed. They didn't have to worry about making a mistake or getting a bad grade. Their journals would not be scrutinized for punctuation and spelling. My purpose was to help my students express and invent whatever came into their minds.

It didn't take long. I began to witness writing that ignored the minimum number of words. Some students were writing 200 to 300 words, impatiently waiting for their turn to read their ideas to the class. They were eager to share and listen to each other. The change was remarkable. Writing wasn't boring after all. Why couldn't we capture and help elaborate the thought level of students? All I needed to do was open the ideas and allow our students a chance to grow.

Do we even appreciate the significance and opportunity that writing provides? It is far more than a form whittled to fit into a given mold. Learning in school is not for a limited period of time; it holds the potential for a lifetime of development. Writing can open a child's mental awareness. It allows a child to evaluate and understand his/her view of the world around them. It encourages a love of fresh ideas and ways of expressing them. It brings up ideas that seemed hidden away. Sitting in a class learning grammar has its place, but does not address the growing problem with education today. Our challenge comes with instilling the inspiration that students need to become all that they were meant to be. We do not want to create a generation of mental robots that helped their school get high scores on tests. Quality writing requires thought and the ability to analyze, all of which are necessary for building our nation's future.

We need a love for originality. We need the drive for the freedom to explore and experience the rewards of self-knowledge. We need to develop the capacity to communicate effectively. We need to understand others and give everyone a voice. Writing develops the depth and inner wisdom that stimulates qualities of individuality.

OBJECTIVES

1) Learning to use writing to express one's feelings.

2) Learning that writing helps to understand others and how they feel.

3) Awakening an appreciation of nature and the world around them.

4) Illustrating their writings and improving drawing skills

5) Learning about the process of putting a book together.

6) Learning about some famous writers and poets.

ACTIVITIES

1) Read poetry: "Where the Sidewalk Ends" and some of Robert Frost including "Stopping by Woods on a Snowy Evening."

2) Go outside and find a quiet place to write – to give students time alone with their thoughts. Have students write about their dreams.

3) Share their ideas with the class.

4) Illustrate their poems and/or ideas.

5) Make a book and have it published.

6) Sell the book for an economic project.

7) Invite an author to come to the class to talk about his/her ideas on how to get a book published.

WRITING IDEAS

A butterfly's journey

How does it feel to be in a chrysalis?

If you were alive in a garden and you were only one inch tall.

My dream is to…

A circus in our planets.

What the world would be like without gravity.

If I could fly.

Halloween on a planet.

If I could change one thing.

If I could re-invent my body.

Write about the biggest cake in the world.

How to celebrate the world's birthday.

Invent a hero.

The discovery of a dinosaur.

Write music with words.

Invent a way to bring peace to our world.

If you could be president what would you do?

Make up a new TV program.

Rewrite a nursery rhyme.

Scribble on a paper then write about it.

If you could live anywhere where would it be?

If you could create a new planet what would it be like?

What quality do you admire most?

How would you make the world better?

What makes America great?

What is wrong with taking drugs?

How would you help a bully?

CHAPTER 15

THE EARLY 1800S

MAIN OBJECTIVE

To inspire students to appreciate the history of our country; to be able to think about other people, and the way they thought and lived 150 years ago.

SPECIFIC ACTIVITIES:

1) Build a dollhouse from a kit with parents' help.

2) Write a weekly diary of a fictitious family living in the 1850s.

3) Decorate the dollhouse and furnish it in the style of the southern plantation.

4) Make butter from cream.

5) Debate from South and North

6) Make a covered wagon with people going west.

7) Make a corn husk doll.

8) Make a quilt by gluing a square paper colored by each student and glued onto a piece of bulletin board paper.

9) Quiz Bowl

10) Field trip to appropriate museum or historic houses.

11) Guest speaker, such as a quilter, to talk about quilts and their history.

MATERIALS:

1) Kit to build a dollhouse

2) Paint

3) Rug samples

4) Materials for drapes and bed spreads

5) Items that can be made into furniture (small boxes, etc.)

6) Glue

7) Scissors

8) Library books such as "Little House on the Prairie," "Grapes of Wrath," first chapter of "Gone with the Wind"

9) Material for a covered wagon

10) Popsicle sticks (for covered wagons)

Doll house in 1800's life-style

SOME DETAILED LEARNING ACTIVITIES 1850

We started out with a family of five —a father, mother, older brother, sister, and a 5-year-old girl. They all live on a beautiful southern plantation. When news comes that there is gold out west, the older boy decides to leave his family and comfortable life in search of gold. His sister marries a man who wants free farm land in Missouri, and she leaves her family for the life of a farmer. The younger daughter stays home with her mother and father. Each week, the class writes about what happens to this family – the problems and successes that they encounter. Everyone writes his/her own story each week. We discuss a different situation before we write the journal: For instance, the hardships of traveling west, the Indians, lawless towns, the railroad, winter, and crossing mountains. These, along with the growing conflicts between the North and South, and slavery, are all subjects that can be talked about. It somehow seems more engaging when students are writing their own stories about this time in history. Of course, the activity could be changed to focus on any part of this time in history.

TREASURE HUNT

It is a beautiful day in 2018. The world is happy. Flowers are blooming and you are taking a walk outside in the mountains of New Hampshire. You come across a dark cave and wander in to see what might be inside. A strange bearded man is sitting next to a big rock. He does not look like he is from this world. We speak to him, and he doesn't answer. We look around and see some hay and some old boots. It is hard to believe, but this man resembles Rip Van Winkle. He has no concept of our clothes – a girl in shorts? A boy in sandals? He had slept for over 150 years. He wasn't sure he wanted to wake up. Where would he go? Where would he live?

We help him down a small pathway and bring him to our summer cottage. We begin to tell him about all the changes that took place while he slept. We need to go out and bring him proof that he had slept for 150 years. He needs to see how life has changed.

1) You need to find a pen and write any sentence with it, to show him that you can use it to write with.

2) You find a lot of things that he wouldn't know. You need to tell him about them, but the letters are all mixed up – you need to unscramble words such as television, computer, telephone automobile, microwave oven.

3) The man seems scared. You decide to sing him a song. Write a song of at least eight lines. Every other line needs to rhyme. Your song should be written to the tune of "Rock-a-Bye Baby," and your whole group needs to sing it together.

4) You find a book for the man. Tell why you picked the one you did. Write your answer down on a piece of paper.

5) You think it is important to ask the man if he has any questions. He does. Write down his questions and your answers.

6) It is time to let someone else meet this man. What is his name? Who will you introduce him to?

7) Before you leave, you see that the man is very weak. You need to fix him a good dinner. Draw a picture of the dinner you make for him.

8) You think that there are new words that people in the 1850s would not know. Make a list of five words you need to let the man know. For instance, United Nations, submarine, etc...

9) The man does not know about our money. Show him the dollar bill with Washington's picture. Draw the coins and one other bill.

10) Look through a magazine or newspaper and pick out seven things for the man to see.

11) Put all your things together on paper and label them for the man.

RESEARCH PAPERS

1) Research quilts and how they were made in the 1800s.

2) Research the clothing styles and tell how people dressed. This could include hats and children's clothing.

3) Research household items that are no longer in use. Tell what replaced them. How did the changes help the way we live?

4) Research the way we spend our spare time. Do you think it is good or not so good?

5) Research schools and how they have changed. Name some good things about both and tell which you like best.

6) Research the food people used to eat and the food we eat today. Which do you think is better?

7) Research the ways people have celebrated holidays. How are they different today? Which do you like better?

8) Research the gold rush. What would you do if you lived in the 1800s?

9) Research the way women lived in the 1800s. What is good and what is not good? How has it changed, and how do you think it will change in the future?

10) Research transportation and how it changed from 1850-1920.

11) Research the life of a child. How did a child's life differ from the way children live today? What is good, and what is not as good? Which do you like better?

12) Research the problems that black people had after the Civil War. How could we have made things easier for them?

13) Research the money in the 1800s. Compare the cost of a car in 1910 to a car today, and a house in 1850 and one today. What makes things so expensive today?

CREATIVE PROJECTS

1) Make a catalog of clothing for women, men, and children of the 1800s.

2) Write an original story about a family living in the 1800s.

3) Draw a picture of a farm in the year 1800 and one in 1980. How are they different?

4) Create a musical instrument and write a song that would be a Negro spiritual and a song that a white plantation owner would sing.

5) Make a quilt out of paper squares.

6) Design a car of the future and be ready to tell the class about the changes you would make from the cars today.

7) The jobs we have today and the jobs that people used to have are very different. What new jobs will we have in the future? Make a chart to compare the different occupations. How do you think the future will change the way we live today?

8) Create a game about life in the 1800s. It should have a board and include facts that we have learned in class.

9) Draw a Christmas scene of 1800 and one of today. How are they different?

10) Make a diorama of a scene depicting the 1800s.

11) If you were suddenly whisked into a time machine and taken back to the 1800s, where would you find yourself? Write a story about your adventure.

12) If you could be someone famous that lived in the 1800s, who would you be and what would you do? Draw a comic book and tell us all about it.

13) If you could change something in the history of our country, what would it be? Write about it.

14) If you could take one thing and re-make it, what would it be? Make your item with the changes and be ready to tell the class how it would change the way people live today.

CHAPTER 16

EMBRYOLOGY

I first became interested in embryology through the 4-H Club. Eventually, I taught a class for them. We incubated chickens for over 10 years, and never grew tired of the learning opportunities it offered. When you are having fun, learning is inevitable. What could be more exciting and joyous than watching a chicken hatch from a shell and getting to hold a soft, fluffy baby chick in your hands? This popular lesson was part of our gifted program spring agenda. Everyone loved it and looked forward to the baby chickens that would appear and teach so many lessons in so many ways. The possibilities were endless and could be fit into the strengths and personal interests of every individual teacher. Here are some suggestions:

1) Space: food supply on a space ship. Write about the chicken from outer space, from Mars, etc.

2) Art: draw chickens and make musical instruments to compose chicken music. Write a rap song about chickens. Do a chicken dance. Write a poem about a chicken.

3) Inventions: the invention of the incubator and turner. Invent a safe home for the chickens, where they will never be bored.

4) Geography: learn about chickens and how they are treated worldwide. How can we do better food distribution? Write a story about a chicken from Spain.

5) Creative writing: the story of an egg. What happened to the germinal disk named Ted? Make and illustrate a book.

6) Animals: learn about the chicken industry. How are eggs distributed, labeled, and treated?

7) Math: look at numbers found at an average farm. When is incubation? To begin this unit, you will need an incubator. I would recommend that you purchase one that is clear plastic so students can easily watch the chickens when they begin to hatch. There are things you can buy to save money on incubators, but I would not recommend this. You want this activity to be successful, and only the best will do. You can also purchase an egg turner and a candling light. Everything can be purchased online. The automatic turner is not a necessity, but I would recommend that you get one when you buy your incubator. You need it to fit and to work together. Because I had a classroom of students, I got a large, 18-egg incubator that cost over $200. With the turner, the cost was about $300. The money was available to me through our economic project. You could write a grant or ask for donations from parents.

ORDERING CHICKENS

You can find many different poultry farms on the internet, many of which ship individual orders of eggs. It is amazing to learn about all the different colors and feather varieties of chickens that are available. It is tempting to order the unusual chicken eggs, but there is a problem with this. You must think beyond the hatching to where your young chicks will go to live permanently. Most chicken owners want chickens for their eggs. The fancy chickens are not good egg layers. If you can find someone who is willing to take your young chicks as pets, you are in luck, and you can order the pretty-feathered birds. But if you are planning on giving your chickens away to someone who wants them for their eggs, you need to get the plain, sweet, yellow-white chickens. The females will have a long-life laying egg. The males will not be so lucky. It is very difficult to tell the males from the females when they are young. You can also order duck or quail eggs. All eggs will come in the mail.

LOCAL LAWS

Be aware of local laws concerning farm animals. Many towns and cities do not allow chickens to be kept, and you do not want to disobey the law by giving the chickens to someone who is not legally allowed to keep them.

PREPARING FOR YOUR EGGS

Be sure you have your incubator all set up before the eggs come. The temperature in the incubator should between 100 and 102 degrees. The chickens will not survive anything above 102. The more expensive incubators are much more dependable and consistent in maintaining a constant temperature.

You will also need water. I purchased distilled water. Tap water will form a crust that is very hard to remove. You need enough water to keep the air moist, but not so much water that the air is too humid. The eggs should never sit in water. There should be a thermostat inside the incubator, which will enable you to check the heat and humidity. Be very careful to place the incubator away from a draft or a window with sunlight, which will alter the temperature and destabilize air circulation. You also need to place the incubator in a spot where students can see but not touch. There have been times when a student turned up the thermometer, and other times when they turned it down, with disastrous results.

TURNING

Pick a time to do this project when there is no vacation to cause an interruption. You don't want your chickens hatching when there is no school. It takes twenty-one days for chickens to hatch. Incubate the eggs so that they will hatch during the week and not on a weekend.

HATCHING

All eggs will not hatch on the same day or at the same speed. Give them two or three days to hatch. Let your custodian know you are doing this project so he is aware of what is going on. If you have an automatic turner, your life will be easier. The only thing you will need to do is keep an eye on the thermostat and make sure that there is enough water to maintain the right degree of humidity. Stop the turner on the eighteenth day of incubation. Put up a chart for the class to see how the chickens develop day to day. I also make a copy of the chart for each child.

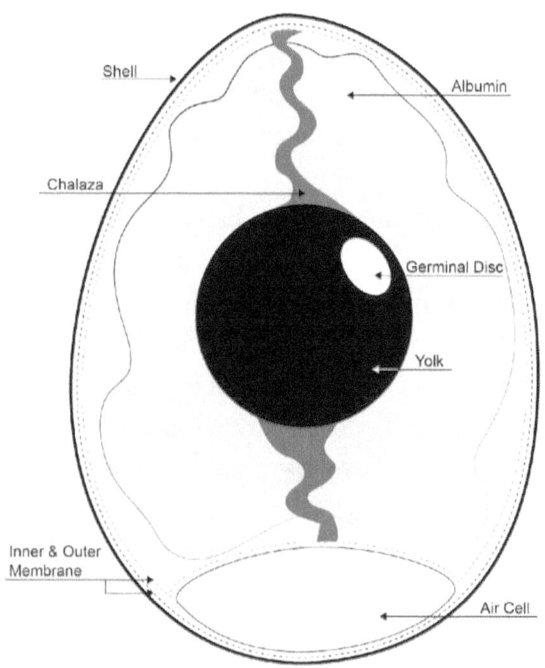

One of the first activities we did was to break open an egg, one purchased from a grocery store. I put one egg on each table, with extras to spare. We broke the eggs open and emptied the contents into a bowl. Each child had a picture of the egg, and we labeled all the parts together. The thin skin acts like a filter and keeps any harmful air from getting at the chick. The shell allows air to enter the egg, and acts as a protection from bumps. Explain all this to the children as they observe their eggs and label their parts. Some students will have trouble finding the germinal disk. It may be on the bottom part of the yolk, so you may have to help them turn the yolk over. Sometimes the yolk breaks; you will be happy you bought some extra eggs.

Once you have put your eggs in the incubator, you have 21 days before you have chickens. That time will go fast! Make sure you do this when the hatching is convenient – not during testing or spring break or some other school event. I always did it in the spring, a month before school was out. It was at a time when students were looking forward to summer vacation, and school was getting tiresome. This kept everyone alert and interested. It was a time to look forward to.

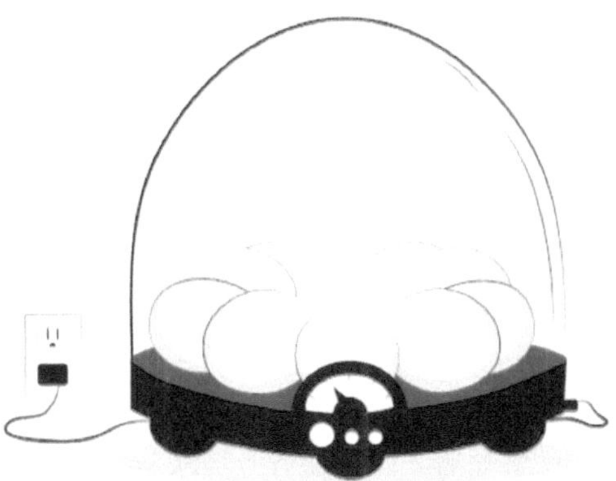

CANDLING

This is amazing. You can buy a small, intense light. Turn the lights off in the classroom. Hold the light next to the egg and watch the chicken moving. The students will be amazed. This is also important to do because some of the eggs might not be alive, and unfortunately, some may die in the incubation process. You do not want a dead embryo exploding in your incubator. How do you tell if the embryo has died? It will turn black and fail to move or grow. This is also a good reason to number each egg. You can keep track of each egg individually and remove eggs if necessary. It is not unusual for an embryo to die. Do not take it personally and blame yourself. It happens. Do not, however, remove an egg too quickly. There have been times when I thought there was no life in a shell, and then was pleasantly surprised when it hatched into a lively chick. It is better to err on the side of caution than to jump to conclusions.

DEATH

This brings us to the problem of death. Prepare yourself and your class for the fact that some chicks will not live. Explain that to your class. Do not allow them to name the eggs or to get attached to a certain number on an egg. Keep the incubation process as general as possible. It is better to candle the eggs after a week, but before the last week. The chickens will get so big that they will fill the egg and it will be hard to see anything but a dark shadow. You, however, should keep a close watch for any problems. Some students would love to open an egg that has died to see what is inside. I could never do that, but did allow students to take an egg to a teacher who was willing to open it.

HATCHING

When eggs have reached the eighteenth day, stop turning them. Put a little more water in the incubator because the humidity will help the chicken come out of its shell. When I first started doing this, I expected the chicken to pop out of the shell effortlessly. I was soon to discover that this was not such an easy process for the young bird.

1) You will hear a small peep inside the shell. I love holding the egg and hearing a sweet peep.

2) A small hole will appear in the egg, and you will see a beak tapping inside. Each chicken is equipped with a pipping tooth that is attached to the top of its beak. This helps the chick break the shell. It will need to tap and break the shell over 1000 times. Difficult as it may be, you cannot help most of the young, healthy chicks. They need to gain the muscle it takes to get out of the shell, so that when they finally break out, they have the strength to survive. This process can take as long as 24 hours. Your class will be a cheering section as they watch. It is hard to do anything else in class when the chickens hatch. When the chicks finally break out of their shells, they will hardly win a beauty contest. They will be wet and unstable. Leave them in the incubator until they have dried and fluffy, as well as stable on their feet.

3) You can remove the shells from the incubator to give the chicks room to move. Sometimes, the newly hatched chickens wobble over to an egg with a chick that has started to work its way out and chirp at it as if to say, "Hurry up! I want you to be my friend."

4) Hard decisions: When there is an egg that has pipped a hole in its shell but does not hatch — you hear it chirping, and yet no progress is being made – you have a choice. Decide to just let it die, or when you are alone, peel the shell away from the chicken, small pieces at a time, to see if it can take over with your help. If you see a lot of blood, there is a problem. Sometimes, the chicken is attached to its shell. The egg white has almost glued the chicken down, But the chicken is perfectly healthy. It just needs to be freed from its shell. In such cases, you can put a little water between the shell and the chicken. This will loosen the chicken and allow it to work its way free. There have been times when I helped a chicken out of its shell, after it has struggled for two or more days. I have made the personal decision that I would rather give the chicken a moment of freedom and a chance for life than to let it die in its shell. This is something I do alone, without children. It is good to have a good vet around, who is willing to take an ailing baby chick and help it if possible. Of all the joys that come from this project, this is not one of them. But it is part of the process. Prepare yourself. The best

hatch rate I have had is 14 out of 18 eggs. I have had as few as 6 of 18 hatch.

I repeat: please prepare the children for the fact that not all the chickens will hatch.

PROBLEMS WITH SOME CHICKS

Chicks are cute – adorable – wonderfully amazing when they are healthy. However, if there is anything wrong with one, the rest of the chicks will peck at it and kill it if you don't separate it from the rest. I have done this several times and ended up with a healthy young chick, which would not have survived without help.

AFTER THE HATCHING: PREPARATION FOR CHICKS

You need:

1) A big box

2) A light that will attach itself to the box to keep the new chicks warm

3) Newspaper and paper towels

4) A water dish for chickens – their air conductors are on their beaks, and they can easily drown if their water source is too deep. It is helpful to put marbles in the container with the water.

5) Purchase chick food at a feed store. You will need at least 5 pounds. Chickens are messy. If you put their food in a large container, they will step in it and go to the bathroom in it. You can buy special food dishes – they are well worth it.

6) A plastic bag.

I continually add clean sheets of paper toweling to the box. Newspaper is too smooth and chickens cannot get traction to stand securely. Paper toweling is better. A plastic bag should be placed at the bottom of the box, then a layer of newspaper, then paper toweling. At the end of the day, I empty all the dirty paper and put fresh paper in for the night. MAKE SURE THE CUSTODIAN UNDERSTANDS THAT THE LIGHT NEEDS TO BE ON ALL NIGHT. If chickens go to the corners of the box to get away from the light, it is too hot. If chickens gather under the light in a huddle, the light is not hot enough. Keep the light on for 3 or 4 days.

KEEPING THE CHICKS

It is up to you. The local 4-H club picked the chickens up two days after they hatched. That seemed early to me. 4-H is not going to necessarily relieve you of your golden angels. If you plan to keep them over a week, you could let a student take them home for the weekend. Make sure there is a safe place where cats and dogs and young siblings can't hurt them. Talk to the parents about caring for them. You will need to find the chicks a home. There may be a nearby farm or a small chicken ranch near you. Know the local laws; some places allow people to have chickens, and some do not. Some of your students will want to take the chicks home. Some may know someone who has a farm. It is good to make plans before you have a dozen or more baby chicks that you don't know what to do with.

NAMING THE CHICKS

Growing up, my mother called me Marilyn. My friends called me Lynn. At camp, I was called Sparrow. In other words, I had many names. We color coded the chicks with watercolor pens. Then, each child was free to name any chicken any name s/he wanted. So, a chicken with a green dot could be Ben, Sally, Tom, Joan, or whatever a child wanted to name it. This eliminated the drama of who got to name whom.

STUDENTS AND CHICKENS

PLEASE REMEMBER TO HAVE EACH CHILD WASH HIS/HER HANDS BEFORE AND AFTER HANDLING CHICKS. Teach children how to gently hold the chicks: Thumb under the head, fingers wrapped loosely around its back, with the other hand under its feet.

Chickens make a lot of noise in their box. To quiet them down, put a large poster board over the top of the box. This will silence the peeping, and it will also stop them from jumping out of the box. We had fun building chick houses from cardboard.

Prepare students for chickens to go to the bathroom because it will happen, and if they are not prepared, they will react with screams. The whole class will laugh and get out of control. I always have a piece of paper towel for the chick to stand on – just in case such an unpleasant event takes place.

Holding a new newly hatched chick

Each chicken has its own personality. This is obvious, even when candling them in the egg before they hatch. Some are lively, and some are easy to hold. These little chicks are great on the school's morning announcements if televised throughout the school. This project belongs to the school, and it is fun to share with everyone who is interested. I opened my classroom after school so that students who were not in my class could come in and hold a chick. We also invited other classes to see the chicks. A few members of our class explained the process to the visiting children. This dominated the attention of the whole school.

Once you have given the chicks away to their permanent residences, you will miss them. But at the same time, you will be glad to finally see them go. We once had a parent who brought in a large cage on wheels. He wanted to see what our chicks looked like when they were adults. He kept one chicken. This parent came every morning, wheeled the cage outside to the shade, and then brought it back to my room at night. It didn't take long before the soft yellow fluff turned to white feathers. One morning, before the students arrived, this young chicken started to make some weird gurgling sounds. This continued for a couple of mornings, until the gurgling turned into a bright, well-formed "cock-a-doodle-do." We had a full-grown rooster who found a happy home near our school as a beloved pet.

Learning is a wonderful thing when you can involve your students in a project so exciting and fun. It teaches them —how chickens grow — the parts of the egg —the time of incubation — many new vocabulary words — to care for and value animals —to respect the welfare of animals —to be creative —to share and honor the ideas of others —to see that other living things have to work hard —we cannot always help chickens, and we should not expect others to do things for us —we should be willing to work hard, too —public speaking skills.

WRITING OPPORTUNITIES

Students can write stories about a chicken's adventure inside the egg, getting out, and after it hatches. Students can learn about the egg industry, and how eggs are distributed throughout the U.S. They can learn how chickens are treated and cared for and learn about cage free chickens.

MATH

How many chickens – 1,000,000. How they are washed, boxed, and weighed. The ideas are endless. You can get relevant videos from the library.

MAKE A MOVIE TO SHARE

When you can involve your students in a project that they love and are excited about, you have found the secret of success in teaching. The students learn because they want to. They are eager to come to class and anxious to get involved. There is nothing more rewarding than sharing with them and feeling the joy of being part of seeing new life and learning how to care for it all. It brings magical moments to a classroom – moments I wouldn't trade for anything.

CHAPTER **17**

MANNERS

With a world of sports teams and after school activities, families rarely sit down to a table set properly. They almost never sit at a table to have a conversation without the television on or the constant temptation to text a friend on their iPad. Life today is very different from the life seniors remember experiencing as they were growing up in the 50s and 60s. While change is inevitable and isn't necessarily wrong or right, it reflects the circumstances of the times in which we live. The world of etiquette, while seeming far removed from daily life, is still in vogue. Anyone who wants to climb the social ladder to success in our world would do himself/herself a favor by learning some basic rules for setting a table, making conversation, shaking hands, dressing properly, and writing thank you notes. It's basic to good manners.

Gifted children will be heading for circumstances where their knowledge of etiquette will serve them well. Classes on manners are offered by various organizations for a fee. Students can avoid the time and money it takes to enroll these in classes if you teach basic etiquette in the classroom.

1) Handshake

2) Table setting

3) General table manners and conduct

4) Appropriate behavior

5) Conversation

This unit is taken up at the end of the day in September and continues through December, one day a week. I include it with the communications and inventions unit.

After we have completed the unit, we have a formal dinner party at an upscale restaurant or country club— it varies according to your resources. Sometimes there may be a parent that belongs to a country club. Sometimes a parent could have connections with a restaurant that offers a formal dining experience. You need to have your own connections. When I have spoken with the person in charge of group dinners, I was careful to make our requirements mandatory.

It takes some convincing to teach good manners to someone who eats delivered pizza while watching "Captain Underpants," but it is worth the effort. The day will almost surely come when students and their parents will thank you for this unit. I have listed some basic skills that everyone should know, but there are many more. You will find books on the subject in the library and on DVDs as well. They are fun and helpful.

When you have been invited out to dinner, it is always nice to ask if you can bring something. If not, you may still choose to bring something extra, like flowers or a box of candy. It is not a good idea to bring food unless asked to do so specifically. If the hostess has planned a nice dinner of roast beef and you bring a cabbage dish, it will be embarrassing for her to refuse your dish even though it will not complement the meal she has prepared. It is always appreciated when a thank you note comes in the mail after a party.

Encourage students to get into the habit of writing thank you notes. Keep a stack of them handy. Teach the students to begin by thanking the hostess, and end the note with a positive remark about being part of the party and being invited to their home. Sign it sincerely, gratefully, yours truly, or something similar. It doesn't have to be long or wordy. It just needs to be sincere. It is a nice thing to do.

MAIN OBJECTIVE

To help students learn how to eat at a table, to dine at a formal restaurant; also, how to act, introduce someone, and generally behave in public.

SUCCESSFUL ACTIVITIES

1) Make a placemat and silverware, plates, cups, and glasses.

2) Role play phone conversations and different social situations.

3) Set a table – place the salad plate, soup spoon, glass, etc.

4) Watch a video on manners.

5) Take turns giving firm handshakes while looking someone in the eye.

6) Quiz Bowl.

EXTRA MATERIALS:

1) Construction paper

2) Scissors

3) Glue

4) Play phone

5) Book on manners.

GUEST SPEAKERS

A social person at a restaurant to talk about the importance of manners.

FIELD TRIP

Formal dinner at a nice restaurant or country club.

BASIC THINGS TO REMEMBER

Silverware: Always start from the outside and go in toward the plate if not sure which piece is right to use for a course.

1) Salad plate goes to the left, above the forks.

2) Glass is above spoons and knife.

3) Napkin goes under forks or on the dinner plate.

4) Dessert spoon or fork goes above the dinner plate.

5) Do not sit down until everyone else does.

6) If grace will be said, wait to put your napkin on your lap. If there will not be grace, put your napkin on your lap right after you sit down. If you need to go to the restroom, place the napkin on the seat of your chair, not on the table, and excuse yourself. When you have finished your meal, place your napkin on the left of your plate. Do not put it on your plate, where it could get grease or food on it, and that would not be pleasant for the waiter who must pick it up. Never blow your nose into a napkin.

7) Do not start eating until everyone has their food. Wait for the hostess to pick up her spoon or fork before you pick up yours. The host or hostess is the leader.

8) Put butter on your butter plate, and break your roll into three separate pieces, one at a time. Butter each piece as you eat it.

9) Keep your arms to your side. Elbows on the table are rude and take up space.

10) Always say please if you need something and thank you when you receive it. Never grab across the table.

11) When a plate is being passed around, do not grab the biggest piece, and do not touch a couple of pieces before you make a final decision. Take the first one you touch.

12) What if you absolutely hate sweet potatoes, and there they are, right on your plate? What do you do? If you are not uncontrollably allergic to the food, try a little helping and try to suffer through it. It isn't polite to tell someone you don't like what they prepared for your pleasure.

13) You should cut one piece of meat at a time and eat it before cutting the next. Your knife should be held in your right hand. After you cut the meat, put the knife down on the right side of the plate.

CONVERSATION

Don't talk about yourself. Find out about others. Listen to them. Ask questions. Good things to talk about are:

1) Families

2) Sports

3) Hobbies

4) T.V. programs

5) School

6) Pets

7) Occupations

Formal dinner

THINGS NOT TO TALK ABOUT:

1) Politics

2) Making judgmental remarks

3) Your personal problems

4) Religion

5) Things you don't want

When talking to others, you do not want the conversation to be about you. You want to get to know people and learn from them. When you talk to them, be a good listener and don't dominate the conversation. Speak in a tone that can be heard, but will not be too loud or so soft that others won't know what you are saying. If you see someone sitting quietly, and you think s/he may be feeling left out, ask her/him a question to bring the person into the conversation. It is not a good idea to talk about topics that will cause disagreements and hard feelings. There are many things to talk about that will be pleasant and meaningful at the same time.

SHAKING HANDS: SECRET TO SUCCESS

When you first meet someone, remember these important steps:

1) Hold a person's hand firmly – don't squeeze it and don't offer a loose, floppy, spineless hand. The way you grasp someone's hand tells a lot about what you think about yourself and what you think about the person you are meeting. A firm hold shows self-confidence, determination, and dependability.

2) Look the person straight in the eye. Don't look away – to the floor or ceiling – you want the person to know you are giving them your full attention, and you consider them important and of value. Meeting someone eye-to-eye enables you to connect with them and shows your ability to be sincere and honest.

You may have to practice this several times, saying "How do you do" or "It's very nice to meet you." Then say, Mr.___________ or Ms.___________; or, if they are your age, you can call them by first name. Listen for the way you are introduced to get the clue as to what to say. This is a VERY IMPORTANT gesture. One CEO mentioned that he didn't hire anyone who didn't know how to shake hands, so learning this is a secret to success. It makes a good first impression and may even get you your dream job. When your meeting is over, you can say, "It was nice to meet you." You may need to practice this several times.

DINNERS

MANDATORY REQUIREMENTS

- Pay no more than $15.00 a person including tax. This was a challenge, but we managed to do it.

- Give everyone a choice of chicken, beef, fish, or a vegetarian dish.

The rest of the meal, which included soup, salad, roll, and dessert was the same for everyone. Some years we got larger portions than others. What we sometimes ended up with was a child's portion. This left some parents a little hungry, but it kept our prices down and served our purpose.

Each place setting needed to include a drinking glass, a salad fork next to the dinner fork, and a soup spoon next to the teaspoon. We also needed to have a bread plate and a knife along with a cloth napkin and tablecloth.

The boys needed to wear a tie and dress shirt. The girls wore a dressy outfit, which could include a pantsuit.

We collected the money and choice of entre a few weeks before the dinner. We made place cards or name tags for each person, which was color coded to correspond with their choice of dinner. Beef was red, chicken was green, fish was pink, and veggie was purple. This system made it easier for the waiter to know how to serve each person.

We had a spot to check everyone in before we went into the dining area. This helped the students stay together without running around unsupervised. We went into the eating area together. We did not have assigned seating. Many parents were interested in sitting together, and I wanted to give them that freedom. Some of the students wanted to sit independently without their parents, and that was perfectly acceptable as well.

This was a holiday party because the decorations in December are especially nice and made the whole scene more festive. You will need to discuss table decorations or centerpieces. Sometimes restaurants provide them; other times you will need to bring them. We had separate tables or one long table. I prefer one long table. This lets everyone feel like they belong together.

Weekend prices are higher. It is better to plan this party on a weeknight when the restaurant is not too busy. You need to make your reservation in September for December and call several times to confirm. You may want to bring a sound system or ask the restaurant if they have one you could use to play soft background music during dinner. I would suggest that you have someone say a simple grace, as well. Students should be instructed not to begin eating before grace. They should also know better than to put their napkins in their laps until grace is said. Just before dessert you may want the principal to speak, and you may want to thank those who helped, plus offer some personal remarks, as well.

This event is special. It is a night students are on their best behavior and excited to try out their newly acquired manners.

MANNERS AT THE TABLE

Give the students the following quiz a week before the dinner party.

1) When you are introduced to someone what should you do and what should you say?

2) What do you say when you leave a person you have just met?

3) When should you let someone know that he/she didn't use good manners?

4) Name four things to remember when going to a party.

5) What do you do if you don't like the food?

6) When you are finished with your dinner, what do you do with your napkin?

7) What do you do with your soup spoon?

8) What do you do with your knife?

9) How do you eat your bread?

10) When someone passes you a plate of full food, what should you do?

11) When you sit down at the table, when do you start to eat?

12) You put your napkin on your lap first unless someone will say _________(grace) first.

13) What should you do if you drop a fork or knife?

14) What do you say if you want to leave the table before everyone is finished?

CHAPTER 18

ECONOMIC PROJECTS

This unit gave my students an opportunity to take charge and become active in making their own decisions. It enabled their leadership skills and self-directed life skills to develop with a new enthusiasm for learning. Many children who were less than involved with school became excited and took part with a whole new attitude.

This unit let the class create their own company, name it, design a logo along with a slogan, make the product, market the product, and then sell it and decide how to use the profit for their class.

My role was to guide their decisions, to help them execute their ideas in profitable ways, ensuring that everyone was being fair, honest, and helpful.

LIST OF ACTIVITIES

ELECTION OF OFFICERS

The students wanting to hold office had to come to class with a written speech to read in front of the class. If they didn't have a speech prepared and written before class, they were ineligible to run. We had small pieces of paper that were presented as ballots. Once everyone heard the speeches and voted, I would choose two people to count the votes.

Once the president was chosen, he/she would preside over the remaining officers being elected in the same way we had elected the president. The other officers were vice-president, secretary, and treasurer.

PRODUCT TO BE MADE AND SOLD

The students were asked to bring ideas and products they had made to our next meeting. I also brought my own ideas. I told the class they had to consider the cost of making their products. They also had to think about how easy it would be to make several hundred.

We discussed our goals including how much money they wanted to make and how they wanted to spend the profit. A few times the class wanted to make something I knew would be difficult to sell, but I let the class decide against my better judgement. However, I also included another idea I knew would be successful. I was not willing to let them fail to make a point. Two such ideas were bracelets made with colored threads and wallets made out of duct tape. They both took too long to make, and only a few students had the patience to make them. Also, the prices would never be equal to the time and materials involved.

Once we decided on the products, they had to come up with a name, slogan, and a logo. We discussed the term brainstorming and began to write down their ideas on the board, emphasizing that nothing was wrong, too silly, or stupid. Anything and everything was acceptable.

We had wonderful ideas and voted for the top three, and then for the top two. I emphasized that the name should be catchy and preferably something that would rhyme. Once the name was decided on, we were done for that week.

I introduced vocabulary words for the class to look up in the dictionary. Here is a list of some of the words: brainstorm, gross profit, net profit, advertising, free enterprise system, tax, proprietor, cooperation and partnership. The next activity included a guest speaker from Junior Achievement. He came into our class and talked about starting a business.

ADVERTISING

Discuss what advertising means and what it does. There are videos that talk about advertising. If you can find one, it can be a welcome introduction. I prepared some posters depicting different kinds of ads.

Emotion/Sympathy – making you feel sorry.
Bandwagon – everyone does it.
Cost – big, free, half off, etc.
Celebrity – using a famous person.
Funny – makes you laugh.
Need – makes you feel you need it.
Food – hunger.
Gimmick – something fun, a prize.

Discuss each ad type and show examples from magazines and newspapers. Ask which ones go best with the products they are selling and the age of their buyers. Discuss popular slogans and logos. Provide each table with paper, scissors, glue, and some of the product they are going to make. Instruct each table to come up with an ad using one of the ad types discussed in class for a happy meal box. Table one then gives their presentation. The class then guesses which ad type they used. After each table gives their presentation, the president asks the class to come up with slogans and logos and the vice-president writes them on the board. The class votes on the one they think would help sell the most product. Because there is not enough time during the school day to make the product, pass out permission slips to stay after school until 6:00. . for three nights to do so.

THE NEXT WEEK

The students have chosen a product, named it, and have come up with a slogan and logo. Discuss mass production and unit production. Split the class into two groups. One group will mass produce the product; the other group will make the product individually. Ask the class which method they think will work best for their class. Set the room up into two groups. At the end of a half hour, see which group made the most and produced the highest quality. Ask both groups what they liked and didn't like about their method. Discuss what would be the best method for the class.

The quality of product is very important. You cannot sell something if it does not look good or hold together well. You need quality control people (stress this). I have found that some students need to work by themselves and others love groups. You can decide how to organize your class. I let the class organize themselves, and it worked very well.

If the class voted to make more than one product, have them make the first product one night and the second product on the second night. This helps to keep everything focused. The class will need encouragement. Pizza is a big incentive. We voted on the place to order the pizza, and each students brought $3.00 to help pay for it,

The treasurer collected the money. I kept extra cash on hand because students often forget to bring money.

COST SURVEY

Ask the students to create a survey for the student body. The survey should include a sample of the product and question asking if they would buy it and for how much. ($1; $2; $3).

During a class meeting, share the survey results and vote on the price. Consider the cost of making the product and the profit the students want to make. A few examples: Students wanted to buy a color copying machine priced at $500; they wanted to have a celebration dinner at a nearby Japanese restaurant for $150. They needed money left over for the class, which would be put away for the economic project the following year.

We discussed net profit and gross profit. How much would the materials cost? Could we cut costs by asking parents to donate things? The answer was yes.

In order to make enough money, we needed more than $1500 net profit. That made the pricing more important. If we charged $1.50, we could make our goal more easily, but would the students/faculty/ staff members at school pay $1.50? That is where our survey helped. The students wanted to try $1.25, they voted on that. In order to make $1,500 we would need to sell over 1000 items; that was a big order.

We knew we had our work cut out for us. I donated a lot of the materials, and we used money that was already in our account from the previous year. Parents also helped.

Once the items you want to sell are made, inspected for quality, and inventoried, you are ready to meet the world. Posters had to be made (not too heavy otherwise they fall).

Flyers needed to go home. Announcements needed to be written, so they could be read with the school's morning announcements.

The next step: Students broke into groups. One group made the posters. One group worked on flyers on the computers. Another group wrote ads for the announcements. Discuss how to make successful big letters, one color.

Once the posters are done, they need to be put up. Use masking tape in circles inside out (so it is sticky all around) and put it on all corners and in the middle of each poster. Press the posters to keep them from falling from the wall. It is better to pick an inside area. The flyers should include information telling where things will be sold and how much each will cost. Announcements can be divided among class members who are interested. The students need to practice so they can read them with a clear convincing attitude. It is good to have more than one announcement.

E-mail faculty asking if students can come at a certain time to their classroom to introduce their product. The class was broken into groups that were, in turn, assigned a specific grade to do. This was an incredible way to motivate the students to buy our products. It was less than an hour and we had the whole school covered. Students handed out flyers when they entered each class.

We were ready for sales to begin. We could have sold our things outside, but it would have been too time consuming to take everything outside, and there was always a chance of rain. We arranged the tables in my classroom so the customers could go to a table and choose the product they wanted to buy. We put a sign on each table with the price in clear sight. The traffic flowed to the door where the students stood to collect the money.

Our class was blasted with customers. The room was so crowded with people we had to line them up outside. Money was toppling out of the cash box. Clearly, our classroom was the place to visit.

MONEY AND PRODUCT

We had lots of money, more than our cash box could hold. At the end of the day the treasurer counted everything and we took it to the secretary to deposit into our account. I was very careful not to let this project disturb the teachers or learning in the classroom. The teachers in turn cooperated with us. The money we made helped us fund projects throughout the year. We were far from rich, but we were very comfortable.

WHAT AND HOW

Some ideas we had through the years.

Goo
Stress Balls
Sparkling Water
Bread Dough Figures
Houses
Puff Balls
Books

After our successful fundraiser and economic unit was completed, we bought our color printer and had a delightful dinner at a Japanese restaurant, all expenses paid. The parents joined us for the evening, and they paid for themselves. The students loved doing this. It taught them many lessons and helped them learn how to work together for a common goal and to experience the joys of making real money.

SOME OF THE MORE SUCCESSFUL PRODUCTS

By far the goo or slime was the most successful. We made it every year because it sold so well. We made it with Elmer's Glue All (not school glue) and mixed it with water and Borax. We put the slime in small containers used for things like tartar sauce or salad dressings, and they were perfect. (For various recipes and information GOOGLE "slime.")

The other students loved this and would come to buy ten or more at a time. We made it with food coloring, so we had many alluring colors to choose from. Over the many years we sold this, we made over $10,000. What made it so easy was that we didn't need to worry about quality control, it was so easy to make, and the kids loved making it.

Making slime

Another popular item to make/sell was the little Puff Ball characters. We gave them different names throughout the years.

SUPPLIES NEEDED:
    Puff Balls
    Wiggly Eyes
    Glue
    Feathers
    Sticky Shapes
    Ribbon

Pipe Cleaners
Sequins

The students came up with many original characters. They needed to be made with enough glue to hold them together. They could be mass produced, but the work needed to be carefully inspected to keep the quality intact.

Once we made the little characters, they had to have a home. We bought Styrofoam food containers at the same store where we got the goo containers. These containers were divided into sections (containers for taking uneaten food home from a restaurant). These made great houses for the puff balls.

SUPPLIES NEEDED
Self-drying clay
Sequins
Paint pens
Glue
Material
Small spools
Tiny boxes
Hair rollers
Bottle caps
Buttons

The idea to make houses came from the children. They made tables, beds, etc. They decorated these houses in wonderful creative ways. We couldn't make them fast enough, and they took time to make well.

STRESS BALLS

Oh, what a mess. Wonderful, but very messy. I ordered balloons with faces on them and the kids filled them with flour.

SUPPLIES NEEDED
>Balloons
>Flour
>Roller
>Plastic spoon

Divide the students into groups of two, one to stick a hair roller onto the top of the balloon and hold it as the other spoons flour into the balloon. Each balloon needed one cup of flour. Once the flour was in the balloon, it was tied and ready to go. The kids loved this, too, but be prepared for flour to be everywhere. I would recommend doing this outside on a towel or blanket.

WATER BOTTLES

Collect these. You will need at least 100. Fill them with water and add sparkles. Supplies needed:

>Water bottles
>Sparkles
>Glue gun
>Food coloring
>Option: mineral oil or white oil

This is another easy one, no worries about quality. Once a bottle is filled with water and sparkles are added, I put the glue gun on the rim and sealed the top on the bottle to stop anyone from opening it.

Another option is to fill the bottle with two-thirds cup water and one-half cup of mineral oil. Add a little food coloring and seal with a glue gun. This is esthetically pleasing and demonstrates that oil and water do not mix. The liquid in the bottles resembles waves when turned sideways. It also demonstrates that water is heavier than oil.

BREAD DOUGH

Probably the most difficult to control regarding quality, but a good option if you are working with artistic children.

SUPPLIES NEEDED
  Elmer's glue
  White bread
  Borax
  Magnets
  Tooth pics
  Garlic press

Mix the white bread with Elmer's glue sprinkled with Borax to retard any bugs. GOOGL "Bread Dough Crafts" for more information. You can create original figures. We got magnets and glued them onto the bottom for either the refrigerator or for magnetized toys that could chase each other. The dough can also be used in the houses.

SERVICE PROJECTS

Gifted students are given a lot of attention. They are looked up to by their peers and family members. They grow up knowing they are smart. Generally speaking, gifted students feel good about who they are. In many cases, these young people grow up in a world that is centered on them and their accomplishments. It is wonderful to feel confident and self-assured. As a teacher of these exceptional children, I felt obligated to help them become aware of the world beyond their own. If I didn't help my students to become more caring and concerned about others, I would be doing them a disservice and depriving those who could benefit from their gifts. It was important to help instill a desire to be of service to a world hungering for the answers that would help solve the problems we face today and in our future.

With this goal in mind, I assigned each student a project for the year. I provided the children with ideas to explore, but allowed them to choose a topic that was meaningful to them.

We based the projects on our topic of study for the year. When we studied animals, we centered on living things. Many students helped in the local Humane Society. We also contributed to organizations that helped endangered species and supporting stray animals.

When we studied geography, we joined organizations that supported children around the world, such as UNICEF, or other worldwide causes such as hunger and women's issues.

When we studied space, we concentrated on dreams that we could help come true. We helped the elderly, children with disabilities, the McDonald House, and the environment.

When we studied art, we worked on bringing beauty to our earth, planting gardens, sending artwork to nursing homes, etc.

When we studied inventions, we encouraged students to invent new things and ways of helping others.

I gave the students a year to work on their service projects. I set deadlines throughout this time to make sure everyone was working on their project and not leaving it to the last minute. On the final day of school, students brought their projects to class to share. The students were not required to write a report about their projects, but they were asked to bring pictures or proof of their work. I wasn't interested in a research work for this assignment. The important thing to me was the project itself. I can never tell you the joy and inspiration that glowed throughout the gifted classroom on the day these projects were shared. It was my favorite day of the year. Some of the most impressive projects involved the whole family. The students were responsible, but could not have completed their service projects without the help and support of their parents.

Services that were provided:

Blankets were donated to animal shelters.

Letters were written to send to veterans overseas.

Elderly neighbors were helped.

Needed items were collected for people in natural disasters.

Vegetable gardens were planted and crops were given to needy families.

We participated in beach cleanups.

Stuffed animals were collected for children who were victims of abuse or fires.

Gifts for blind children were made.

We helped children with deaf parents learn to speak.

Flower gardens were planted in downtown Safety Harbor.

Food banks received contributions.

Dinners were prepared for the McDonald House.

Looking back over the 27 years I taught the Gifted Program at Safety Harbor, I can see how privileged I was to have had the opportunity to teach many moral lessons in life. My deepest, most earnest wish would be that I helped instill in my students a concern for the welfare of humanity along with a sincere conviction to improve the quality of life for all living things. In my mind, there is nothing more basic to the success and happiness of students than for them to have a caring, loving heart.

CHAPTER 20

HOLIDAY PARTY

If you want to enjoy a day with your class or group, this is a wonderful way to celebrate the holidays without too much work on the day of the party.

THINGS YOU WILL NEED FOR THE PARTY

This is a busy time of year. I sent out notices to the parents listing the items needed for the holiday party. However, I always had extra of everything in case we ran out of something.

THINGS YOU WILL NEED FOR THE TALENT SHOW
Karaoke machine with CD Player and microphone
Holiday CDs
Name tags for adults

THINGS YOU WILL NEED FOR LUNCH
Paper plates
Punch bowl
Place mats
Ladle
Canada Dry ginger ale
Raspberry sherbet (1/2 gallon)

Oranges (One for each member of your class)
Sharp knife
Straight peppermint sticks
Chips
Cookies
Fruit
Large garbage bags
Paper cups
Napkins

THINGS YOU WILL NEED TO MAKE THE CANDY HOUSES
Assorted candy– M&Ms, sprinkles, life savers, gum drops, graham crackers (optional)
Styrofoam boxes
Glue Gun
Permanent marker
Paper towel rolls
Milk cartons
Small boxes
Royal icing for the frosting
Confectionery sugar
Plastic knives
Large spoon
Tin foil or large plastic bags

THINGS YOU WILL NEED FOR THE DECORATIONS
Plastic table cloths or bulletin board paper
Construction paper for the placemats
Snowflakes (children love to make them)

THINGS YOU WILL NEED FOR THE GIFT EXCHANGE
Homemade gifts

THINGS TO DO BEFORE THE PARTY

MAKE THE FROSTING

You will need Royal Icing, which can be purchased at any store that sells cake decorating materials. It comes in a can and is a powder you mix with powdered sugar and water. It is expensive if you are using enough for 100 students. The advantage of using the powder is to avoid egg whites. Uncooked egg whites are considered unsafe. Royal Icing is far better than the frosting you can buy in the grocery store because that never hardens. Royal Icing hardens like a rock and will hold decorations firmly in place. It is messy and requires a strong mixer. After many years of making a mess in our kitchen, I got smart. I asked our cafeteria manager to help, and she was happy to do so. She had a giant mixer and we made all we needed for the week in one morning. I asked her to order the confectionary sugar from her source. She did so and charged it to my account.

I came in early one morning before school and we made the icing. I never took her help for granted. I made sure I mopped up the mess when we finished. We sealed everything with plastic wrap so no air could get in and placed it in the school's large walk in refrigerator.

If you do not have this kind of help, you will need to make the icing at home the night before. Make sure it is in an air tight container and kept refrigerated overnight. When you bring it to school the next day it should be refrigerated. Make a lot—more than you think you will need. It is always better to have some left over than to not have enough.

CONFECTIONARY SUGAR

You will need a lot. The directions on the Royal icing can are self-explanatory. It depends on how many children you will need it for. We got over 24 pounds for 100 students.

THINGS TO DO ON PARTY DAY WITH THE STUDENTS BEFORE PARENTS ARRIVE

Before the parents arrive, put the raspberry sherbet in the freezer and the Canada Dry Ginger Ale in the refrigerator. Pass out scissors and have the children select Styrofoam containers and/or boxes, which they will then shape into their houses. When we studied space, we made rockets; when we studied geography, we made gingerbread houses. Glue gun each house to its personally named plate and put aside for later. Children who finish early help decorate the room, cover the tables with bulletin board paper, and make place mats for the tables. Cut out slips of paper and number them numerically for the talent show.

TALENT SHOW

Choose a student to act as the master of ceremonies for the talent show. Prepare numbered slips of paper and have each child take one to determine the order in which they will perform. Create an ordered list of performers listing each name with its corresponding talent. Give the list to the master of ceremonies. If any of the children do not have an act, have them tell a joke or read a poem. Every child must do something for the talent show. Make sure that each act does not require a lot of preparation, so the show flows smoothly. It is helpful to do a quick run through prior to the parents' arrival.

WHAT TO DO WHEN PARENTS ARRIVE

When the parents/guardians arrive, have the children escort them to their seats. Have the master of ceremonies turn on the karaoke machine for the microphone. After welcoming the parents, he/she announces the acts in numerical order. During the talent show, if a parent has not arrived by the time his/her child is ready to perform, be flexible and let the next student perform.

LUNCH

After the talent show, I prepared the punch by combining two one-liter bottles of cold Canada Dry Ginger Ale with one-half gallon of raspberry sherbet. I opened the cookies and snacks and prepared the oranges by cutting an "X" on the top of each one and inserting a peppermint candy stick inside. (For best results use straight peppermint sticks, which are thicker and more porous than regular candy canes.) As the children pressed the outside of the oranges and sucked the peppermint sticks, a delicious peppermint-flavored orange juice came through. As the children went to buy their lunches or opened their lunch boxes with their parents, we turned on Christmas music, which included "The Nutcracker Suite" by Tchaikovsky and traditional music from all faiths.

When they were ready, the students came up to get some chips, punch, and the much-anticipated oranges. A parent also went to the cafeteria to get a pan of frosting. After lunch we cleaned up, leaving the bulletin board paper on each table.

DECORATE THE CANDY HOUSES

Pass out the houses to each student and discuss the design, balance, and planning. Make sure to have some pictures of the houses to share and point out what was used to make a door or a window. Discuss patterns, expectations, and how their houses should be planned. Mention that if they just plop candy all over without an organized plan, their houses would not be as good to look at as one that was thought out. I often told them that a home builder didn't lump windows or doors in a pile; he had a plan.

Put the frosting on a plate placing one on each table with plastic knives. Have the class cover their houses with the frosting, which must be thick enough to support the candy and decorations. It is important that the houses are all covered with frosting before you put the candy on the table because the children will want to start putting the candy on before they have finished covering the houses, resulting in half-finished houses.

Creating a candy house masterpiece

You may have to help some students do this. When you are discussing the houses and how to put them together, parents can help by sorting out the candy and putting it on the plates, to be set aside until everyone is ready. We used to put graham crackers on the frosting to make the houses, but they became soft. The houses looked great with just the frosting and candy. You can make the choice. It will take a while for the houses to dry and get hard. I let them sit before covering them with tinfoil or a plastic bag, which is easier to carry.

Clean up is easy; remove any salvageable candy from each table and then roll up the table covering and put it in the garbage. Of course, the children will want to eat some of the candy. That is part of the fun. Frosting will disappear quickly. Keep your eye out for this so you can replenish the supply. Some students will need help and suggestions. Be ready to encourage and provide the support as needed. Parents love this activity and will enjoy helping. You will need their help to make this activity move along successfully. Encourage the children to be imaginative and original with their ideas.

HOME MADE GIFTS

This is a neat thing to do, but its success depends on how well you orchestrate it.

Start talking about the homemade gifts at the beginning of the year. Mention it at the open house with the parents, so they will start thinking about what their children will make. The potential problem with this is that some students will work for hours making a gift while others will throw something together at the last minute; or even worse, buy a gift. If you prepare everyone way ahead of time, this will help solve the problem.

Make suggestions to the class. Show craft magazines. If they are unable to think of something offer suggestions. Tell them homemade cookies or candies are not permissible.

Remind the class to make generic gifts. If any students he/she want to make something specifically for a boy or girl, have them label their gifts "boy only" or "girl only."

Another thing to consider is religion. If you have non-Christian students, ask the gifts to be for anyone, which would include those who do not celebrate Christmas. Tell them to mark their gifts as "Christmas," "Hanukah" or "neutral."

If you know of any children that lack the money or support to make gifts, you can help them after school using school materials and with your help. Sometimes a parent would be willing to devote the time in helping the child.

THE PARTY DAY

Organize the room so that there is a place for everything. I put the gifts under the table where the candy for the houses is kept. I cover the table so that the gifts are hidden for the day. Once the candy houses are made and the tables are cleaned off, the children come over to the table where their gifts are waiting. They each take their own gift and sit in a large circle. You will have to help them do this as they will wiggle together and the circle concept will be forgotten. This is also a good time to check and see that each student has a gift. If someone does not have a gift he or she will have to step outside the circle and watch. This is a hard lesson and yet it is important for the children to see that they must give in order to receive.

Now you have a big circle of children with a mountain of gifts in the middle just waiting to be opened. This is when you tell them:

The rules of the game:

Pick someone to start. That person gets to pick any gift from the center. Explain that they may not be able to keep the gift they choose. Caution them not to be disappointed if someone takes it away. You can also tell the class that they only know what the gift looks like from the outside. They have no idea what the gift really is. Continue in order. The Students have a choice to pick from the middle or take the first person's gift. If they take the first gift, that child is now able to pick another gift from the middle.

Enjoying their homemade gifts

The third person has the same option. They can take the first or second person's gift or one from the middle. To shorten the process, a gift can be taken only three times. If it has passed hands three times, it becomes frozen and cannot be traded again. It is helpful to have someone keep track of the number of times a gift is taken because it can become very confusing. When everyone has a gift, the person who was last to pick is the first to open their present. Keep the circle intact because everyone will want to see each gift as it is opened. Have someone there to take the wrapping paper and put it in a garbage bag. Make sure each gift is opened, seen, and appreciated before the next gift is opened.

It is important for each gift to be recognized and appreciated. It is also important for the children to think about being kind and not looking disappointed. There will be some fantastic gifts and there is bound to be those who get gifts that are not so fantastic. But you know that is a life lesson. We all must learn to be thoughtful of each other and appreciate the motive and effort of others and not just themselves.

It has been my experience that the children like their individual gifts and are not disappointed. They love sharing how they made their gifts. Homemade gifts are the highlight of the day. They are well worth the time and effort you put into the preparation of this project. In a world of T.V. and video games, it is good to see something that involves imagination, creativity, and thoughtfulness.

The children loved the gifts they got, but even more so, they loved the excitement of giving to one another. Over the years we had some incredible gifts; many were made from kits. Some examples; blankets tied on all four sides, painted bird houses, games, ornaments, scarves, books, scrapbooks, wreaths, tie-dyed shirts and pillow cases, candles, dishes, homemade clay and soap, musical instruments, and treasure boxes. After the gifts were opened and everything cleaned up, I passed out the small gifts I had made for each student.

CHAPTER 21

QUIZ BOWL

At the end of each month we had a quiz bowl, which contained questions specific to the topic we were studying. Review can be fun, exciting, and important to learning. The Quiz Bowl is all these things and more. At the end of every month, we would take an hour to go over some of the most important ideas the class had learned.

1) Prepare small squares of paper. Enough for each person in the class.

2) Write a number between one and five on each square. A class of 25 would have 25 pieces of paper with five ones, five twos, five threes, five fours, and five fives.

3) Fold each paper in half so the number is not visible.

4) Put papers in a hat and pass it around the room so everyone can pick a paper.

5) The number on the paper determines the team the person who holds it is on. For instance, all those who picked a one are on team one.

6) Once everyone knows their team number, they move to a specified part of the room. The fives went to the window, for example, the fours to the front.

7) After each team is together, they need to form a unit with a writer and a captain.

8) Once the teams have decided on a captain and a writer, paper and pencil are passed out.

9) To reiterate, you have five teams: a captain for each team and a writer for each team. Each team has a paper and a pencil.

10) I write on the board Team 1, Team 2, Team 3, etc.

11) Now we are ready to begin. I have a series of questions written down in front of me.

12) I read the first question; each team must decide the answer, and the team writer writes the answer down.

13) Once the answer is written down, the captain stands. The captain is the only one allowed to stand. He cannot change the written answer.

14) We wait for every captain who wants to attempt to answer to stand.

15) We then go to each team, asking them to read their written answer.

16) The teams with the correct answer each get a point on the board.

17) Then the second question is asked in the same way as the first.

18) When I feel we have had enough questions, the team with the most points wins and earns a piece of candy – a simple but satisfying reward.

19) A variation on this would be to have some questions worth more than others. This helps if a team has fallen behind and begins to lose interest.

20) You also may have a tie. Have a tiebreaker only for those teams that are tied.

21) If problems that cause arguments come up within a team, you can take points away. That is a great incentive for them to quiet down and cooperate.

Writing down the answers helps the teams to stay honest. Once they hear someone else's response, there is an obvious tendency to change their own. If it is written down, it cannot be changed.

The students really looked forward to this activity. It was a great review. I did not take questions out, so the students got to know the answers well. I always started with the information from that month's unit of study before I went back into the questions more than one month old.

CHAPTER 22

TREASURE HUNT

"It's the best day of the whole year." "I've been waiting for this day. This time we're coming in first." The treasure hunt was at the end of each year and was highly anticipated.

This activity was earned by hard work and organization. It included team building, logic, and a review of what we had studied during the year. To be eligible for this event, the students had to successfully complete their notebooks. For some students this was easy, but for others it was daunting and took them a while to realize they had to keep track of their papers or they would not be ready to do the treasure hunt. It was torture sitting at a desk doing work when your class was having fun doing the treasure hunt. A hard lesson, but it was very effective. Students made sure they would not experience another year of disappointment when trying to finish their work because they had not completed it on time or kept track of all their papers. I had many parents and students thank me for helping them develop their organizational skills. These were rewarding moments that made the struggles well worth the effort.

We divided the students into teams of four or five. I read the problem or challenge to the class explaining each problem to be completed. It was usually a fictional story based on what we had studied during the year. We discussed strategies. For instance, they might not want their whole team working on the same problem. They had to organize a way to work together and to use their time effectively.

THINGS TO DO
BEFORE THE DAY OF THE TREASURE HUNT

Buy more than enough prizes to go into a treasure box (big enough to hold all the prizes). I would allow each member of the winning team a choice of five prizes; the second-place team four prizes, etc. One of the reasons this activity was successful for 27 years was because the prizes were so sought after by the students. If you purchase cheap prizes from the dollar store, the students will eventually lose interest in the treasure hunt. Make sure the prizes are age-appropriate and well-liked by the students.

Find a hiding place for the treasure. (I always would bury the treasure for the older students) Decide on the code you will use for the puzzle. For the first and second graders, I used pictures. Decide how many challenges there will be for the Treasure Hunt.

Depending on how many challenges there are, divide an 81/2" X 11" piece of paper into that many pieces. Number each piece. Do not number them in order.

Draw the code on top of the puzzle pieces. Make sure each piece has a part of the code.

Make more than enough copies of the puzzle for each team.

Cut out each puzzle piece. Have one copy of the whole page for your master copy.

Have as many envelopes as puzzle pieces.. Number the envelopes, place all the puzzle pieces numbered 1 in envelope #1; puzzle pieces numbered 2 in envelope #2, etc. Always have more puzzle pieces than needed in case one piece is lost.

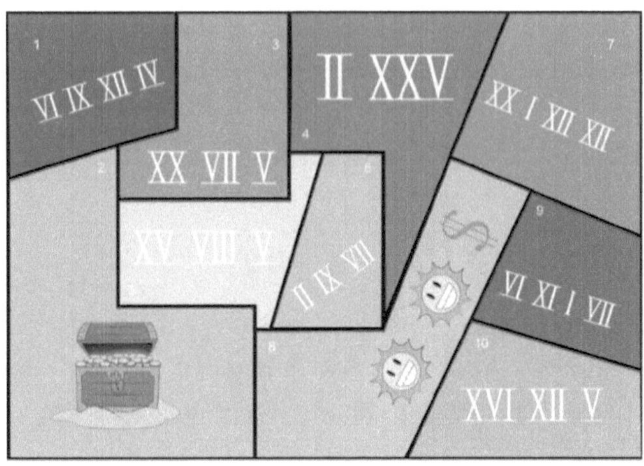

THE TREASURE HUNT

Start the treasure hunt by reading the story. To divide the teams up, I cut out small pieces of paper numbered numerically depending on how many teams would compete. Each student picks a piece of paper with a number, which tells them on which team they will belong. For example, if the student picked #1, they will be on team 1. Each team chooses a captain and a name for their team.

Give the captain the envelope containing a copy of all the challenges. The envelope will also be used to hold all the puzzle pieces the team has earned. Each team decides on a strategy regarding who will work on which challenge. When a challenge is completed, they bring it to me to check. If it is correct, they receive that number puzzle piece. Once all the challenges have been successfully completed, they must clean up their area and return to me for a final check. Then they are given the final puzzle piece, which is necessary to find the treasure. Next, the team must assemble the puzzle and decipher the code, which reveals the location of the treasure. The first team to find the treasure brings it to me and each member chooses five prizes.

Each team had a leader that is responsible for their team envelope. They would also name their team and be responsible for decorating their envelope, which is for the puzzle pieces. No one wants to lose pieces, although you do have extra if you have a problem.

Once a task is accomplished, the team members show me they have completed their work successfully. After I check it, I give them the puzzle number of the task completed. If their work is wrong, half done, or sloppy they have to go back to do it the right way. Students often try to get away with sloppy work, but I never accepted it. Quality is very important.

Next, the students put the piece in their envelope and continue this process until all tasks are completed and all puzzle pieces collected. Before I gave them their final puzzle piece, they had to clean up and come to me for a final check and inventory. I made sure the final piece had all the necessary information; the treasure could not be found without it.

At this point, students started putting puzzle pieces together. Some teams began this task before everything was finished steadfastly staying on task working to figure out the code.

I arrived at school at 6:30AM . and buried the treasure for the 4th and 5th grade. The 3rd grade was hidden somewhere on campus. The 2nd grade had its home with another teacher and the 1st grade's treasure was hidden someplace in our classroom.

I made sure the treasure was worth working for. Oriental Trading offered a variety of enticing toys. A nearby coin shop offered foreign coins and I put in a few dollar bills along with a few candy bars.

This is a wonderful activity. It energizes the students to complete their class work together as a team member. When students who were slow at completing notebooks were finally ready, I allowed them to help a team already formed or I had them start their own team. It all depended on the time and the group.

I would recommend this activity with five stars. It is a winner. Students that learn together are highly motivated. It is the kind of activity that encourages learning and helps the students to love school as well. Examples of specific treasure hunts can be found at the end of each yearly subject.

Figuring out the puzzle for the treasure hunt

CHAPTER 23

PARENT CONFERENCES

One of the most helpful activities the students took part in was the student-parent conferences, which we held twice each year. Parents visited our classroom and looked over their children's work with their child. We did this once at the beginning of the year and once at the end of the year. The first conference introduced parents to the school year and enabled them to see how their child was performing in class. This enabled parents to see any potential problems and to identify ways they could work to overcome issues that needed to be addressed. It also gave parents the opportunity to encourage and compliment their child on the good work they were doing.

The conference held at the end of the year gave students the opportunity to go over their work with their parents and show what they had learned. It was an exciting time of pride as the children were proud to showcase their accomplishments and take charge of the conference with their parents. These special meetings made a big difference to my students. They knew their parents would be looking at their work, and they wanted to make sure everything they did was worthy of praise. It was not easy organizing these notebooks. The process enabled the students to learn some important skills that helped them in many ways in the future.

- It made them accountable.

- It helped them to be responsible for their work.

- It helped them keep things in order and to keep track of their work.

- It showed them the consequences of being unorganized, and it showed them how much work it took to re-do lost conference papers. It gave them the incentive to keep up with their work on a weekly basis.

- It developed communication skills as each child explained their work to their parents.

- It helped the parents and the children come together to discuss the kind of progress they had made and how to support each other in achieving their goals. It helped students' self-image as they were encouraged and complimented by their parents.

- It helped the students evaluate themselves and it formed a desire to improve their work.

- It helped families feel welcome in the gifted classroom and to come together as a cooperating unit as they talked and shared their ideas and/or problems.

- It gave me a chance to observe relationships and interact with the families.

- It often was an opportunity to discuss problems and ideas I would never have known about under other circumstances.

I created a checklist, which included all the work we had finished during the year. As students went through their notebooks, they checked off each page and put it in order and in the right section. If they were missing anything, they were responsible for re-doing it. They got a certain number of points for each page and for overall neatness. They added up their points and the total gave them their grade. Any notebook with an A or B was acceptable; anything below a B was not, and the student had to go back to the drawing board and re-do some pages or improve on neatness. A C-grade was unacceptable. It was average and I never wanted them to be satisfied with just getting by. An average attitude was a lazy one, and they could do better.

In addition, students needed partners to go over the checklist and double check to see if it was correct. This helped the students work together and evaluate someone else's work and compare it to his/her own.

Preparing for conferences was not easy for the students. I helped when it seemed overwhelming. Keep in mind, for many students it was a work in progress. It took a couple of years for some students to catch on. Every notebook (three-ring binder) had five dividers: Vocabulary, math, main subject, puzzles and logic, and creative. After each section was put in order, students created title pages, wrote introductions, autobiographies, their own table of contents, and at the end a conclusion and an index. We also included their research reports. The finished notebook was comfortably full, the pages were in order, and each page numbered for the index, which was an opportunity for students to review their year's work. When these notebooks were completed, they represented the year's effort and were masterpieces, which were kept for years to come.

Before the parents arrived for any conference, students filled out an evaluation sheet they would share with their parents.

There were some concerns with this very valuable activity. Some parents did not come to a conference. It didn't appear that they valued their importance. The children of these parents did not have the opportunity to share their notebooks, and thus did not receive the encouragement and support that really made a difference in student's attitudes. At our school, the gifted program is not included on the report card, and therefore students in the program did not have the incentive of a grade to motivate their desire for excellence like they did in the regular classroom. In the cases where parents didn't come in, I let the student go to their classroom to share their work, and on rare occasions, I let the book go home. The book never returned in the same condition it was in when it left. It seems that spilled milk, dogs, or younger siblings bore the blame. When parents care, their children care, and it can make all the difference. I would adamantly encourage every parent to learn as much as possible about your child and his/her education. For each conference, I asked parents to bring healthy snacks while I brought paper products and drinks.

Each parent received a small pack of papers to fill out during the conference. These papers helped everyone focus on the relevant topics studied that year. I included a blank paper for parents to write a letter to their child complimenting them on how proud they were of their child's progress. I included a few sample letters to give parents to read in order to understand what was expected of them. These letters were invaluable and cherished by students.

The students were given a paper notifying the parents of the conference two weeks in advance and then again a few days before the conference. The notification was by written note on each student's homework. The conference started right after school and lasted until 6:30AM. It was a long day, but it was only two days a year and well worth it. The togetherness and unity created in these conferences were indispensable for our growth.

Before the parents arrived for the conferences, I gave each student the following form to fill out:

1) Something I am most proud of and why.

2) How could I improve?

3) Three things I learned.
    A.)

    B.)

    C.)

4) The thing I like best about myself in this claas.

STUDENT EVALUATION FORM

1) What did you learn from this conference?

2) What did you like the best?

3) What was hard for you?

4) What lessons did you learn?

5) How will this help you in school?

6) How will this help you in life?

7) Did you do your best?

8) How would you do this differently if you did it again?

9) How do you see yourself as a learner?

10) How would you grade yourself and why?

11) Who did most of the talking?

12) I could tell what I learned.

13) The grade I think I got.

14) I went through my work easily.

15) My work was neat.

16) My work was organized.

17) What more do I want to learn from this subject?

18) Did I make eye contact with my parents?

19) Did I take charge or did I let my parents talk?

20) Did I feel comfortable? If not, why?

21) Did I like Gifted? Why or why not?

22) How can my parents help me?

23) How can I help myself?

24) How do I learn best? Drawing or writing?

PARENT EVALUATION FORM

One thing I learned about my child was

I would like to see Ms. Wickstrom help my child with....

STUDENT-PARENT CONFERENCE RUBRIC

To be filled out by the student

Name_________________________ Date_________________

Peer Evaluator (Parent) _________________________________

Student Parent

1) Is your portfolio well organized and neat?

2) Did you explain what you have studied from the beginning of the semester up to the present?

3) Do you have good study skills?

4) Were you honest and sincere in your delivery?

5) Were you able to answer all the questions?

6) Did you ask your parents how they might help you reach your goals?

7) Did you thank your parents for attending?

8) Did you return your portfolio to its proper place?

9) Did you plan for how you can improve and be a better quality student?

"Q" for QUALITY

"C" for COMPETENT

"NY" for NOT YET

(Include a handwritten letter from parent to student)

Dear _____________,

Thank you for inviting me to your gifted classroom for this wonderful conference. I am so proud of you and all that you have done. You are learning skills that will help you all through school. I am especially pleased with your attitude towards learning and helping our world. You are special to me and I love you very much.

CHAPTER 24

FIELD TRIPS AND GUEST SPEAKERS

Field trips are wonderful ways to learn. I tried to schedule two trips every semester for each of my classes and they loved it. With over 500 excursions under my belt, I learned a lot about places to go and how to get there. This chapter will give anyone planning a trip some important tips, which will help save you time and trouble. Through the years I have come to value the experiences that field trips provide. They help bring families together, they open doorways to knowledge, and offer new ways of seeing the world. They are incredible resources, which inspire new ideas and awaken dormant interests and possibilities for students and their parents.

1) Make sure the field trip is on the school system's approved list. If it is not, find out what you can do to have it included.

2) Fill out all the necessary paperwork. You may need several approvals for the trip.

3) Decide if you are going to use parent drivers or get a bus. If you use a bus, be prepared for the extra money it will cost.

A.) Check with the office to see which bus lines are on an approved list.

B.) Call for quotes, the prices will vary.

C.) Reserve the bus at the beginning of the year. People reserve buses in advance, and you could find all the buses are taken if you wait until the last minute. Check and recheck with the bus company a couple of weeks ahead of time to confirm your day and time for the trip. Sometimes they forget or don't have you on their list.

COST

1) Your school should have a special fund for students who need financial help.

2) You usually get one free ticket for every ten paying students. I used this "free ticket" to help students needing financial help.

3) You could hold a fundraiser to help with the cost.

4) A parent could donate money towards the total cost or simply pay for a student needing financial help.

MEDICATIONS

Check for any problems with motion sickness, medications, etc. It is much easier if a parent accompanies a child with a medical problem. If this is not possible, keep medications with someone you know is dependable. Make sure they have your cell phone number in case a problem should arise. You should carry all necessary medications with proper instructions. Check this out at least a week before your trip.

DRIVERS

1) Ensure that all drivers are approved to drive.

2) If children need car seats, ask the parents to bring them. Make sure names are on each chair and return them promptly after the trip.

3) Have the students whose parents are driving choose one person they would like to come with them.

BUSES

Make sure the bus has a bathroom, air conditioning, and a DVD player. Have specified students bring preapproved movies to play on the bus. This helps keep the students occupied and in their seats.

1) Have students bring books to read or games to play.

2) Put names on everything; stress that often. They cannot share iPads.

3) Bring a sweater in case the air-conditioning is too cold.

4) Ensure the bus is new, if possible.

5) Buses are different sizes and carry different numbers of passengers. There is a big price difference between a 45 and a 55-passenger bus.

6) Do not allow students to eat on the bus unless the bus company approves it.

7) Let students know they are responsible for keeping their space clean.

8) Have a garbage bag and pass it around before you get off the bus.

9) Check if the bus has a microphone. It is good to be heard if you want to talk to the group.

10) Take attendance.

11) Let the parents know they are helping and spread them throughout the bus. Don't let them sit together and ignore the students. You need to make this point before the trip.

12) Make sure you mark your bus so you can identify it when it is time to go home.

13) Check to make sure the bus is the same one coming and going so the kids can leave their things on the bus while on their trip.

Each driver or chaperone should have a packet. Inside should be a list of students to watch during the day along with:

A.) Name tags for each student in a group.

B.) The schedule for the day.

C.) Cell phone of the teacher in charge.

D.) Map if necessary.

E.) A thank you note for their help.

Giving each chaperone the name tags to pass out to their group is helpful because each child will know who their chaperone is, and the chaperone knows and can recognize the students they will be watching for the day. Ask a parent to let you know if a child is late or absent. If everyone has a name tag, everyone has connected with their chaperone. Name tags do not take the place of attendance. Once on the bus, take attendance to check and make sure everyone is there. Some teachers do a number count, which works, but taking attendance ensures that everyone is on the bus. Do this each time your group gets on and off a bus.

I do not give any chaperone more than four students. If there are not enough parents to keep the numbers at four, I try to get more parents to help. Parent-chaperones need to enjoy their day. If they are keeping track of eight or ten children, it can be hectic, and the chances are they won't volunteer for the next field trip. I found it much easier to leave myself free for the day. This gives me the freedom to solve any problems that may come up. If I have a group of students, I am obligated to take them around and therefore do not have the ability to keep the whole group working well. I see my role as a supervisor on field trips.

Be prepared for little glitches. Keep a positive attitude and never let a child feel like a problem. You are there to support your students and parents.

MONEY

Some field trips are expensive. I decided that I wouldn't let that stop me. What I emphasized was the educational value of the trip. We had fundraisers and had students come up with ways to raise money on their own. I gave parents months to raise the money. I asked for donations from parents at our open house at the beginning of the year. One year I was given a check for over $1,000 for tickets to the Nutcracker Ballet. Another mother helped finance a trip using money she had received from her mother's estate, stating that her mother would want her to use the money for the school. Nothing was impossible.

If money is a problem, the school should have money available to help students who need financial support. No children should be denied the opportunity to attend a field trip due to financial reasons.

BEHAVIOR ON FIELD TRIPS

Students know they are to behave on field trips. Instruct students to stay in their groups and obey their chaperones. If they act out or wander off by themselves, they will not be able to attend another field trip. I am very strict about this. Students who do not follow rules put everyone at risk and take away the learning opportunities of the whole group. If a student misbehaves, I allow them to attend the next trip, but only if their parent goes with them. Throughout all the years and field trips we attended, I only had to say no to one student. There were several times when the parents had to attend. When you provide experiences students look forward to, discipline is generally not a problem.

MONEY AND GIFT SHOPS

I allow students a chance to go to the gift shop. We do this at the end of the trip, which the students really enjoy. Limit their time and make them understand they can only spend the amount of money allotted. I let each student keep track of their own money. If you are on a time schedule, make sure students are not holding up the bus because they are in the gift shop. For some, this is one of the first times they have had money to spend without their parents. It is a learning experience in and of itself. I don't tell them what to buy, but I do not allow students to play machines with their money, I make that clear. Their time and money should be better spent on learning or buying something they can take home.

COMMUNICATION

Have a designated parent that can be contacted if the bus will be late. This can happen for a variety of reasons. Traffic can be heavy; an accident can hold up traffic. A student group could have been late coming on the bus. There are many reasons why a bus would be late. You do not want a crowd of concerned and fearful parents anxiously waiting for their child's return. Communication is essential to everyone.

EXCEPTIONAL CIRCUMSTANCES
1)   Someone needs to leave early.

2)   A relative will pick them up.

3) A student gets sick on the trip.

4) A medical problem arises.

5) Something is lost.

6) A student does not have their things such as a sleeping bag, money for food, or the chaperone suddenly cannot attend.

LOCAL FIELD TRIPS
    A.) Art
    B.) Insects and Animals
    C.) Geography
    D.) Inventions
    E.) Manners
    F.) Oceans
    G.) Space
    H.) Communication

Listed below are specific field trips. The letter following the trip indicates the subject. Example 1) Art Museum – A = Art

1) Art Museum – A

2) Dali Museum – A

3) Clearwater Aquarium – F

4) Ruth Eckerd Hall – A

5) MahaffeyTheater – A

6) Tampa Theater – A

7) TampaArt Museum – A

8) Theater – Mars – Planetarium – G

9) Tampa Aquarium – F

10) T.V. Station – H

11) Tarpon Springs Sponge Docks – C and F

12) Busch Gardens – C and B

13) Restaurants – E and C

14) Tea Rooms – C

15) Science Museum – B

16) Art Galley – A

17) Multicultural Fair – C

OUT OF TOWN (OVERNIGHT POSSIBLE):
1) Kennedy Space Center – G

2) Sea World – F

3) Universal Studios – H

4) Disney – H

5) Epcot (scavenger hunt) – C

6) Thomas Edison Museum – D

7) Disney Hollywood Studios (scavenger hunt) – H and D

8) Phosphate mines – B

9) Bishop Planetarium – G

10) Ringling Museum Sarasota – A

11) Lego Land – A

Never underestimate the value of field trips. The children and parents love them. In many ways they were the highlights of the year. The final trip which was for all my classes came at the end of the year. It usually involved an overnight excursion and buses. We would have over 100 people on these trips. It was a lot of fun, but it took good organization and a willingness to spend hours outside of school to get everything together. I was more than grateful to put these trips together because I knew how much fun everyone would have and the memories would be enjoyed for years to come. The learning made lasting impressions for a lifetime and helped build a foundation for future knowledge.

There are so many wonderful opportunities for field trips in the Tampa Bay area. Outside of this area look for museums and historical places. If you don't find obvious venues you can be creative. For instance, a train ride would be fun and offers educational history regarding the way trains work today. I talked to the children's director at a local art museum where classes are taught about paintings and sculptures. We put together a wonderful overnight adventure where students did paintings, drawings, sculptures, and drama—putting on a short skit. We also made musical instruments with visiting daytime instructors. The kids had a great time and the museum offered this to other groups after seeing the potential for future programing.

Scavenger hunts using cameras reinforce learning in specific topics that create learning in places not often thought of as educational. For instance, a local park is a great place to discover insects and little creatures or plants that are often overlooked.

Cape Kenedy

Busch Garens

Feeding the dolphins at Sea World

CREATIVE FIELD TRIPS

1) A trip to clean up a local area; collecting litter and making a list that tells about the people who go there.

2) Humane Society; Go on a tour. Hold the animals and bring blankets.

3) Newspaper factory.

4) A local factory or business that allows students to go on a tour.

5) McDonald's or a fast food restaurant.

6) Hospitals; collect books, hats, and stuffed animals.

7) A grocery store can be fascinating. List all the places around the world that bring food to the store, and then later look the places up on a map. How do they keep things cold and fresh?

8) Nursing Homes; make flowers to give out, sing songs.

9) A florist or garden store, showing different plants.

10) A sewer facility; how water is cleaned and reclaimed.

11) A nearby theater; behind the scenes tour.

12) A local farm.

The list is endless and exciting. Work with the sponsors to ensure a safe, rewarding, and educational event. Places like the Kennedy Space Center or Busch Gardens are experienced in group work and will not need your help. You may need to tell them some specific things you want your students to learn, but once you arrive, you can relax and let the employees take over. On these trips, your work is in organizing the trip and making sure all the permission slips are in, etc. Once everyone is there, you can turn over the reins and be part of your group.

1) A good trip is finding a place to plant trees to help the environment. Research wildlife, urban growth, and loss of habitat.

2) Making signs for voting and visiting a local precinct to learn the procedures in their county. No specific names or party should be mentioned. This can help students value their democracy and the importance of voting.

3) A local bank could teach students about saving money, writing checks, credit cards, etc.

4) Visita local college and tour different parts of the campus. Encourage the value of education and student possibilities for the future.

5) Visit a courtroom and see how it works with the judge and lawyers.

6) Post offices are interesting to see how the mail is organized and sent out to homes and businesses.

7) A local police station emphasizing the importance of obeying the law. A policeman's job of keeping everyone safe.

8) Fire department

9) Local artist, inventor, musician would also be good choices.

If you are going someplace that does not usually have visitors, you may have to plan your trip carefully with the person in charge. Suggest that the guide be child friendly and flexible. You should have specific things in mind that you want your students to learn. Don't expect anything; make sure you go over every detail before the trip. It is a good idea to visit the place beforehand to introduce yourself and look around for potential issues and or interesting things you would like to see or talk about. Research the purpose of the place in order to make the most of your trip. Prepare your students before the trip, so they are ready, interested, and excited about what they are going to learn.

GUEST SPEAKERS

1) <u>People from different countries</u> – there are ethnic groups that love to talk to students. See if there is a local club or organization that has people from different countries and work together.

2) <u>A U.N. Representative</u> – contact them or local representatives.

3) <u>UNICEF</u> – contact them for a speaker, they may have a local representative.

4) <u>Peace Corp</u> – contact a representative.

5) <u>Service Groups</u> – locate them on the internet, contact a local representative.

6) <u>Environment</u> – world pollution and how to deal with it. College professor may want to talk.

7) <u>Holocaust Museums</u> – have speakers that are available.

8) <u>The Deaf</u> – find a place where they have deaf people go. . Invite someone to come and talk to students and show them sign language or braille for the blind. I strongly recommend this.

9) <u>Special Needs Teacher</u> – find a representative for Special Olympics.

10) <u>Store Owner</u> - someone who has their own business. You may have a junior achievement in your area. They love to come out for economic reasons.

11) <u>Artists</u> – find someone in your area that can demonstrate techniques.

12) <u>College Professors</u> – retired or available who can talk about specific art periods.

13) <u>Local Museums</u> – they will often send guest speakers; some museums share art objects for extended periods of time.

14) <u>An Astronaut</u> – they are usually available to talk. If possible, include the whole school.

Know your specific area and search out special speakers who are experts in their field. Guest speakers are wonderful. However, it is important to know, in advance, what they are going to say. If they have any artifacts to bring, it is even better. It takes time to contact some of these people, but it is worth it. Sometimes a parent may have something of value to share with the class.

CHAPTER 25

RUBRICS AND REPORTS

RESEARCH PAPERS

Each year, my students were given a research paper to complete at home and then share with the class. This project was assigned along with a creative project. The subjects related to the topic we were studying for the year. This was a big deal. Parents were responsible for helping their children. The success of any student's project depended largely on the parent's support. It was a rare situation when I had to help a student because the parent was too busy or unable to help.

At the beginning of each year, I passed out directions for this paper along with a list of choices for both the research and creative projects. In the paper, I gave a step by step process that needed to be followed and a rubric that would be used in grading the paper. Most students had computers at home with internet access to information, but I wanted them to learn how to research beyond their computers. The local library had periodicals and books available. It was important to be aware of these resources and to learn how to use them. I also encouraged them to conduct interviews when possible.

This was an opportunity for the children to explore and enjoy learning. The purpose of this assignment was not to complete a paper about a subject; it was for them to discover the journey of new ideas, which would help them form their own ideas and options. They could not receive an A without offering an analysis. It was far too easy to write facts. I wanted them to interpret facts and come to their own conclusions. This paper also taught students to organize information. They had to write an introduction, main part, and conclusion in a logical sequence. Their first job was to pick the subject they wanted to write about. Next, they needed to scout out the information they needed for writing the paper. They were required to keep track of books and resources for their bibliography. I asked them to write down relevant information on cards.

After reading about their subject, students were ready to decide how they intended to organize their ideas. This had to be done in outline form and brought into class for me to check. We spent a couple of weeks in class going over the outline format, so they understood what to do. Checking outlines individually helped me know if the student was on the right track. Once their outline was completed, they were ready to write their sloppy copy, which had to be in their own writing. It was also to be included in their final paper. The sloppy copy let me know they were doing the paper, even if the parent typed the final draft. A title page and bibliography were required, which included at least three different sources from three different locations. They could not all be from a computer or book. I also asked that they turn in their note cards.

The creative project was up to them and did not have any specific instructions. The day the papers were due was exciting. I had a rubric on each table for students to fill out while listening to the reports. These papers checked off the introduction and conclusion. They also wanted to see if the paper had an opinion. There was a small space for a positive remark.

It didn't take me long to see the class struggling to pay attention to students who had soft quiet speaking voices. I bought a karaoke machine, which made it easier to hear everyone. We talked about public speaking and how to use expression when talking. I got a music stand so students could put their papers on it as they held the microphone in their hand. Before the student completed reading their paper and prepared to share their creative project, they asked the class a question about their report. The students raised their hands and the student that got the question right was the next person to give their report and went to the board to write their name and the name of their report. In this manner, the students would be ready to go after the creative report was given; this saved a lot of time. We had someone collect all the rubrics from each person and gave them to the speaker. I filled mine out as well, but mine was longer. When a report was done, I took it so I could check it over and grade it using a rubric for a sloppy copy, research card, title page, bibliography, opinion, introduction, and conclusion.

I did not say much about the creative project because they were open. I graded them on time spent, originality, and neatness. These projects were fun to do and allowed the students to do something showcasing their talents.

The most important goal in doing these papers was to stimulate the students' intellectual curiosity and help them formulate their own opinions and ideas. Many times, a student would complain because they didn't get an A. With the rubric it was easy for them to see why. It helped explain away questions. It was important to include the rubrics on the directions and instructions.

I usually allowed students six weeks to do these papers. The first two weeks they were to come up with a topic, the next two weeks to gather information and bring in the outline, the next week to write a sloppy copy, and the final week to put it all together. Don't let students put this off and try to do it at the last minute. It won't be fun.

HOW TO GIVE REPORTS

It makes a long day to do all the reports at once. I chose to do this because they took up so much time, and I had so many other things to do. But I can see the value in dividing them up into two or three weeks. The fifth graders had one-thousand words, and some of my more ambitious students went way beyond that. I asked the class to reduce the report they were to read to the class to five minutes and turn in the complete report to me. This helped a lot. The younger grades had shorter reports, so it wasn't as much of a problem. Many years after a student has left grade school, I have seen parents who have thanked me for requiring their child to do these reports. They provided a foundation that helped them all the way through college.

GRADING RUBRICS FOR RESEARCH AND CREATIVE REPORTS

RESEARCH REPORT

Neatness, spelling, and punctuation
Title page
Introduction
Main part of paper
Your opinion
Conclusion
Outline
Books and sources of information
Extra things above and beyond requirements
Presentation
Read slowly and audibly
Expression
Correct pronunciation
Knowledge of topic

CREATIVE REPORT

Neatness
Time and thought involved
Imagination and creativity
Exceeded expectations

CHAPTER 26

HELPFUL VOCABULARY AND PROCEDURES

INFORMATION FOR PARENTS

If you are a parent wondering about the process involved in placing your child into the gifted program, you are not alone. Be patient, but not too patient. Find out the procedures that your county follows. You can contact the gifted supervisor in your school district and ask for information regarding placing a child into the gifted program. If your county does not have a gifted supervisor, make an appointment with the gifted teacher or staffing specialist at your child's school. There is no reason for a parent to be kept in the dark about the process. Take control and know just what is going on and what is a reasonable timeframe to wait for everything to be done. This will eliminate frustrations and misunderstandings. Keep in mind that the gifted teacher has many hats to wear. She is responsible for teaching, and all the preparation that goes into that. She is also responsible for testing prospective students and keeping track of the paperwork. Your child is not the only one in the qualifying process. My advice is to be polite, but persistent at the same time.

HELPFUL VOCABULARY

1) Popular Intelligent tests – The Stanford Binet, WISC; Reynolds. Each of these tests evaluates different strengths of the student. The psychologist giving the test would know which one to give each child for best results.

2) LOE – Lack of Eligibility. This means the score on the test given was not high enough for the student to qualify for the Gifted program. Generally, the score should be 130, but this varies from state to state.

3) Partial Score – I find that if your child receives a score that is less than 130 but scores a 130 on one of the two parts of the test, the child can qualify based on the partial score. Each test has a verbal and a non-verbal score. The two scores are averaged together. They usually are close, but there are times when a child gets a 120 verbal score and a 135 non-verbal score. When averaged out, the total would be 126, which is not a score that would qualify them for gifted placement. But because one of the two scores are 130 or more, the child qualifies.

4) Letters of Recommendation – If a child receives a score of 128-129, he is within 2% of the mean and can qualify with three letters of recommendation. The letters can be written by teachers or by someone close to the child. These letters are often the reason a child's final placement is held up. So, if this happens to your child, keep track of who is writing the letters and check that they are written in a timely manner.

5) E.P. Once the gifted teacher receives the paper work from the psychologist, she checks to make sure the score is high enough. If so, she will set up a staffing meeting for you to sign the papers giving your permission for your child to be in the Gifted program. The teacher will prepare the educational plan, which includes

goals and objectives for your child. Read them carefully and do not hesitate to add something you feel would help your child.

6) E.L.P. – This is similar to an E.P. but is for a child who is in more than one special education class.

7) First Notice - you will receive a notice of the meeting with the date and time it will take place. If you cannot come at the designated time, let the teacher know and a new time will be arranged. The first notice should be two weeks in advance of the meeting.

8) Second Notice – you should receive a final reminder for the meeting. Please make every effort to attend this meeting and ask any questions you have. Not every child gets one of these meetings. They are for students in special education programs, and gifted falls within that category. When you come to the meeting, you will see the Gifted teacher, the LEA representative, and the classroom teacher. Find out the supplies needed, the weekly assignment expectations, homework, and upcoming field trips. Also, let the teacher know of any problem or concerns that you have.

9) Report Card – your child will receive two Gifted report cards – one in the fall and another at the end of the school year.

10) Student-Parent Conferences – you will be invited to a Student-Parent conference. These conferences are for you and your child. Your child will have prepared for you to come. S/he will show you his/her work and tell you how s/he feels about his progress in the class. This is not for you to have a conference with the teacher. If you feel you would like to talk to the teacher, arrange a time, but do not use this conference for this purpose. The student-led conferences are very important and your child's work in the Gifted class will maintain a higher quality if the

child knows you will be looking at his/her work, and that you care about the child and what s/he is doing in the Gifted class.

11) Update – every year, or every two or three years - it depends on the state – you will have a meeting with the gifted teacher. At this meeting, the teacher will have new goals and objectives for your approval and signature. You will also have an E.P. update when your child transitions to middle school.

12) Private testing – some parents don't like to wait for the school testing or may just decide to have their child tested themselves. If a teacher has a chance to talk to a parent like this, explain that the psychologist should have approval of the county. Otherwise the test will not be recognized. The school should have a list to give parents. Testing is expensive. Parents should be prepared to pay at least $200. Make sure the test given is approved by the county. If your child was tested by the school and did not qualify you are free to have your child tested again privately with a different intelligence test.

CHAPTER 27

YEAR-END NOTEBOOK CHECK LIST

Research Report Grades	Creative Report Grades
195+ = A+ 190 = A 180 – 185 = B 170 – 175 = C	120+ = A 120 = B 115 = C

Report written in own words (10 points)

___

opposing opinions (30)

___

correct spelling, punctuation, and use of language (10 points)

___

sloppy copy (10)

___

bibliography - at least three sources (10 points))

___

title page (5 points)

____

introduction (10 points)

____

conclusion (20 points)

____

score card scale 0-125 points

____

ORAL COMMUNICATION (5 points each)
spoke loudly and clearly and spoke in a well-paced manner

____

used expression and showed interest in topic

____

maintained eye contact

____

used own words

____

score card scale 0-20 points

____

CREATIVE PROJECT (15 points each)
showed time and effort

____

was creative and showed original ideas

____

was neat and held together well

___

was able to show learning

___

did more than asked

___

score card scale 0-75 points

___

PRESENTATION (10 points each)
Research Creative
was able to share interesting information about topic

___

___

asked a good question about the report

___

___

was comfortable sharing information

___

___

was able to describe project and research work

___

___

did more than asked (+20 points)

___

___

score score

____

____

COMMENTS:

____

____

____

____

____

____

____

____

____

____

CHAPTER 28

CONCLUSION

To me, teaching is the sunshine of life. It feeds the soul and blesses others with a light that reaches beyond one's personal horizons. I wish teachers everywhere could come to feel the freedom and excitement to give and discover creative ways to inspire students—to appreciate each opportunity in every child. Enhancing learning is a gift that is for giving to our world's future - one that is filled with universal compassion and love.

LETTERS

You are so creative, talented, smart, kind, so many words describe you but the word that Stands out the most is "gifted." You have taught me so many things that will help me in my life. You've taught me things that have improved my school education. You were the reason why I always looked forward to going to gifted class. I miss you so very much Mrs. Wickstrom

Words could never express all you have given my children, including first and foremost a deep love of learning. You are by far the best and most respected teacher my children have ever had—by their own accounts, you have molded their minds and their hearts. You will always hold a special place in their hearts and in mine. Thank you so much for your creativity and love.

Thank you Mrs. Wickstrom for all you have done for me. Through the gifted program in my elementary school years you have given me a ton of skills and a wealth of knowledge that I will carry with me for the rest of my life. You have taught me the importance of manners and how to write an outline and research report. You have encouraged me to express my creativity, be curious, and to get involved in helping our local community. You always found ways to make things fun. The Christmas party and the end of the year treasure hunt were always things I looked forward to. My favorite topic we studied was "space, and my favorite field trip was to the Kennedy Space Center. Thank you for being such an outstanding teacher and for being one of the people I look up to and admire most in my life.

I want to thank you for all the things I learned from you. I know that these things are going to stay with me for my whole life. You taught me how important it is to help others and how to be part of a team. I have always loved to write and draw and you taught me that these things are just as important as math and science.

Dear Ms. Wickstrom,

Thank you so much for the orange peppermint stick. When I saw it the fond memories brought tears to my eyes. It was truly special! Thank you for the incredible impact you have had on my life.

Dear Marilyn,

I wish you happiness and contentment. Safety Harbor Elementary was very fortunate to have you as their gifted teacher. You are one of the corner stones of the school. Please remember all the wonderful attitudes you gave your students. You are an awesome lady. God bless you.